SKOAL
SCANDINAVIA

Books by Edward Streeter

DERE MABLE

DAILY EXCEPT SUNDAY

FATHER OF THE BRIDE

SKOAL

SCANDINAVIA

by EDWARD STREETER

Maps and drawings by A. Sheldon Pennoyer

HARPER & BROTHERS, PUBLISHERS, NEW YORK

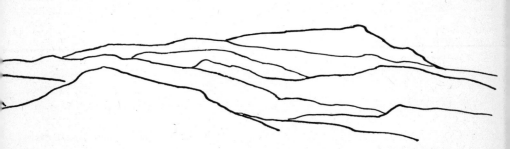

SKOAL SCANDINAVIA

Copyright, 1952, by Edward Streeter
Printed in the United States of America

All rights in this book are reserved. No part of the book may be used or repro-
duced in any manner whatsoever without written permission except in the
case of brief quotations embodied in critical articles and reviews. For information address Harper & Brothers, 49 East 33rd Street, New York 16, N. Y.

FIRST EDITION

B-B

To

SARA AND LUCY AND GEORGE
my peerless traveling companions who are
so happily intertwined in my memory with
all things Scandinavian—

> —*hoping that I may be as favorably
> embedded in their recollections after
> they have read this book.*

Contents

Foreword

THIS IS THE STORY OF FOUR PEOPLE WHO SUDDENLY decided to take an automobile trip around Norway, Sweden and Denmark—a circuit which, for some unaccountable reason, is seldom made by Americans.

It is not a travel book. It makes no attempt to "cover" the Scandinavian countries. There are certain experiences, however, so beautiful, so unusual, so filled with color and contrast, that the temptation to write about them becomes irresistible. Motoring in Scandinavia is at the top of the list.

Most travelers in the northern countries merely touch base by plane, train or boat at Oslo, Bergen, Stockholm and Copenhagen. That is better than not going to Scandinavia at all, but to get the feel of the fjords and the lonely, snow-patched uplands of Norway, of the forests and the blue lakes of Sweden and the ancient villages and thatch-roofed farms of Denmark, one must travel through the country districts—and for that there is no substitute for your own car.

Throughout the book I have used the word "Scandinavia" to include Norway, Sweden and Denmark. Apparently there is no such place. The word at least is not listed in my dictionary, which is very coy on the whole subject. It *does* list the adjective "Scandinavian" which it defines, in the cowardly manner of dictionaries as "of, or pertaining to Scandinavia." Whether or not there is such a word or such a place, however, no one can keep repeating "Norway, Sweden and Denmark," and in any event they were Scandinavia to us.

The principal characters in the story have been disguised a bit with the hope that I may still have a friend left after publication date. The incidents are all true, however, and they have been set down just about as they happened. I only hope that in the process I have not offended any of the good friends who were so kind and hospitable to us while we were in their countries. If I have done so inadvertently, then I hereby tender my humble apologies.

I am quite sure that almost every statement in the following pages will be challenged, in whole or in part, by someone in a much better position to know the facts. The diversity of opinions which we received while planning the trip practically ensures this. All I can say in defense is that these are our impressions and, be they right or wrong, accurate or inaccurate, they are the only impressions we have.

If I seem to have borne down a bit roughly on a few places and people or been indiscreet in expressing opinions about national customs and institutions, I hope that Norwegian, Swedish or Danish readers—should there be any—will bear in mind that there has been no malice in the telling. Our reactions merely reflect the frustrations of four ignorant innocents permitted to wander around loose in strange countries.

Because American automobile travel in Scandinavia is on such a relatively small scale it is sometimes difficult to obtain detailed information of the kind that motorists need. For the benefit of those who want to know *something* about road conditions, itineraries, maps and all that sort of thing—and who do not give a rap about what we thought of *dyner*, sod roofs, crayfish, *snaps* (or, indeed, of one another)—all items of an even vaguely practical nature have been brought together in a "Memorandum to Travelers" at the end of the book.

As is usually the case, the trip would have been far less satisfactory, if not impossible, without the kindly help and guidance of many Norwegians, Swedes and Danes in the United States, and it would also have been far less pleasant and colorful without the warm and open-armed hospitality that was extended to us wherever we went in the Scandinavian countries.

To all who contributed so generously to our pleasure; to the officials of the three Scandinavian Travel Bureaus both in New York and abroad; to the Scandinavian Airlines System, the American Scandinavian Foundation and the AAA, all of whom were so unbelievably patient with us—to all these charming people— SKOAL!

SKOAL
SCANDINAVIA

NIGHT OVER THE ATLANTIC

1

Night over the Atlantic

THERE IS A MOMENT AT THE TAKE-OFF WHEN THE PLANE is neither on the ground nor in the air. For a brief instant of time it hangs between two worlds—poised, temperamental, indecisive.

Then one notes (always with surprise) that a marker beside the runway has begun to grow smaller. A factory building sinks below the window sill. The plane has become definitely committed to a new element.

I felt muscles relax that I had not known were tense. George leaned toward me across the aisle. For a moment I thought the hairs of his mustache were standing straight out—but it was probably the light.

"It reminds me of a trip I took during the war from Dakar to Marzur," he shouted.

"What war?" I shouted.

He let his voice down and I could no longer hear him over the unaccustomed roar of the four great engines.

It didn't matter. George's life was a series of reminders. I knew that during the next fifty days, I would have ample time to catch up with his past.

What *did* matter was the incredible fact that we were on our way to Scandinavia—Sara, Lucy, George and I. We had talked about it for so long—read about it—argued over plans—the odds were so overwhelmingly against four people maintaining their aggregate health long enough to stagger aboard a plane on flying day—that it was hard to believe that the Atlantic Ocean was lurking under the cloud bank below us.

Last February when George had suggested that we ship a car over to Oslo, fly after it and motor through Norway, Sweden and Denmark, the idea had seemed so preposterous that Sara and Lucy had ignored it and gone right on with their discussion about someone in Greenwich who was getting married or divorced or something.

If they had been more attentive the whole thing probably would have died right there. George hates being ignored, however, and Scandinavia gradually became an obsession with him. Before we knew it he had caused it to grow in our consciousness from two vaguely shaped peninsulas to a group of countries with roads and mountains and unpronounceable towns.

Then one evening George had produced a Scandinavian Airlines System flight schedule—and here we were.

It was late afternoon. The plane landed like a feather on the enormous concrete apron of the Gander Airport, and then, forty-five minutes later, we were in the air again, headed out over the Atlantic. This was for keeps and no fooling. Captain Björn Ullebust (Norwegian) sent back his compliments and offered us the Freedom of the Cockpit.

George and I went up somewhat nervously. We were not sure just how to act in the pilot's quarters of a transatlantic plane. I think we expected everyone to jump up and shake hands and that, after the captain had explained everything, there would be salty stories of adventure over the sea.

We were mistaken. No one paid the slightest attention to us. These handsome young men were obviously occupied with running an airplane. The roaring in the nose of the ship was terrific.

Through the forward windows there was nothing to be seen but swirling fog.

Every inch of space was filled with gadgets. It was inconceivable that any one man could learn the purposes of all of them during the course of a normal life. Occasionally Captain Ullebust reached above his head into a nest of switches and turned one without so much as glancing up. Every so often, the engineer officer would lean forward and adjust one of the several levers between the pilots by an eighth of an inch.

Nothing would happen. In an automobile, when you turn switches and push levers, something noticeable happens immediately. If it doesn't, you take the jalopy to a garage. These lads, however, were constantly poking and tweaking at the confusion around them without any appreciable result.

George and I began to feel rather foolish and returned to the more familiar atmosphere of the cabin.

Anne-Lise Franke, our lovely Danish hostess, brought our dinner trays. It was an excellent meal, garnished with a cocktail, beer and a double brandy, followed, insofar as this traveler was concerned, by a double sleeping pill. It was all very relaxing and after Anne-Lise had removed the tray my chair kept tilting further and further back until I was reclining in the lap of a Norwegian sea captain who occupied the seat directly behind me.

Under such circumstances one grows to know people quickly. He was returning to Norway for the first time in forty years, with mixed feelings of anticipation and dread. At the moment, as a professional in the field of transportation, he was much perturbed at the reckless way the airlines handed out food and drink.

"In my passenger ships," he said, "they'd bust the boilers to get 'em in and save a meal. I remember once bein' off Hatteras and radioin' in we'd dock at 9:00 A.M. Right away word came back,

'Forced draft. Dock at seven.' We did it. Nearly shook her plates out, but saved the breakfast."

I put on a pair of slippers and composed myself skeptically for sleep.

Night on a transatlantic plane. In the aisle, the night lights have been turned on—narrow slits of brightness in the gloom. The seats are all tilted back as far as they will go, looking like a column of tin soldiers which have fallen, one against the other. The engines have taken over and fill the cabin with a gigantic, rhythmic lullaby.

After trying conscientiously for an hour to simulate a sleeping passenger, I opened my eyes cautiously and looked about. Apparently, everyone else on the plane was sleeping like an infant. Then, across the aisle, I caught the moist glint of a half-opened eye. It closed immediately like an alarmed clam. Down the aisle, someone shifted position and stuck his head out stealthily to reconnoiter. It was a kind of game in which severe penalties resulted if you were caught awake.

I looked out the window beside me. To my horror, a red glow came from under those tinny-looking flaps just behind the engines which open and shut from time to time like the petals of a modernistic flower. Quite obviously, the engines were white-hot. Undoubtedly a stoppage in an oil line. In a few moments, both starboard engines would either drop out or pour themselves into the sea in the form of molten metal.

What to do? Whom to tell? It seemed silly to ring for Anne-Lise and explain to her that two of the engines were about to disintegrate. In any event if the oil line was plugged it was plugged. We certainly were not going to stop and unplug it in the middle of the Atlantic. I shut my eyes and felt the two sleeping pills take hold, ever so slightly. Who cared about the engines!

To the rear of the cabin, near the exit door, four die-hards stood talking. In any night group there are always three or four super-men who need no sleep and whose greatest pleasure is to spend all night huddled in a small group swapping stories. I dozed and woke up, dozed and woke up again. Each time they were still talking and eventually the sound of their voices merged with the motors and became part of my strange, new world.

Now, ahead of us, the first signs of dawn were visible. The hori-zon had emerged from the darkness and while I watched, a band of sky immediately above it became faintly luminous.

I looked at my watch which was still set at New York time. It was only 11:30 P.M.! Here it was, officially Friday morning, but as far as my inner man was concerned it was bedtime Thursday night. Here was the sun, about to smile through the window of the plane, hoping that everyone had had a good night's rest, when, as a practical matter, the night had been completely chopped out of our lives.

The whole thing became too complicated for me and I fell asleep again.

It was raining hard as we came roaring down through the clouds like a noisy vulture. We were coming in to our second stop—Prestwick, Scotland. Below us, in the dim light, we could make out the east coast of Ireland. Our plane took the Irish Channel like the water jump in the Grand National. A neck of land swam under us which, appropriately enough, was blanketed by a golf course. On the edge of the airport, a group of Scotch cows paused in the midst of an early breakfast of wet grass, to glance at us as our wheels touched the concrete with a squeal.

We taxied to the entrance of a beautiful old manor house whose lighted windows made the drenched murk outside even more dense. It was a quiet, lovely, old house which belonged in the middle of an ancient deer park and should have been surrounded by lush, sheep-cropped turf and venerable oaks. Instead it was surrounded by a lawn of wet concrete on which a flock of great planes were squatting like dejected rooks.

We were rushed through the downpour into a dining room. Young men immediately entered like a chorus, bearing hot coffee and eggs, mounds of marmalade and stacks of leathery toast. They wore full-dress suits, complete to boiled shirts and white ties. It did not seem like the hour, the weather, or the place for formal evening dress.

Speaking of the hour, what hour was it? Everyone had his favorite theory. Some derived pleasure from sticking to New York time. To them this was a kind of midnight snack. The bold, care-free type had set their watches at Oslo time just before leaving New York. Scientific types kept adjusting their watches every few minutes.

George commented on the fact that at home, when there was no difficulty in finding out the time, he didn't give a darn about it. Somehow or other when one began flinging about through space like this, however, the hour suddenly became important. It seemed that the more difficult it was to find out the right time the more one craved to know it. George recalled that once in Matabeleland it had been impossible to ascertain the correct time for weeks and as a result one of the white hunters went off his trolley and tried to kill the cook.

As early-morning table conversation, this sort of talk gave little evidence of elasticity, so we dropped it in favor of criticizing our fellow passengers. There was rich material to work on. Everyone looked a bit cold and leathery like the toast—with the startling exception of the air crews. These young gods and goddesses sat together in eager groups, chatting, laughing, and eating as if they had just finished a nine-hour sleep.

A young man came up to our table. "My name is Sven Bock," he said, "I am the public-relations man. We're glad to see you in Prestwick. Did you have a good night's rest?" He sat down and looked at us—eagerly—as if it really mattered. He was so full of energy, so hospitable, so friendly. Outside, the dawn continued its struggle to pierce the double blanket of Scotch clouds. We suddenly felt very tired, very old.

I had looked forward for weeks to our first sight of the Norwegian coast. After leaving Prestwick, we had bored up through the rain and were now traveling a few thousand feet above a dense cloud bank that extended to the horizon like a frozen sea of jagged ice floes from which the sun bounced back with painful brilliance.

The loud-speaker above our heads gave a preliminary cackle and the voice of Captain Ullebust announced: "We are over the coast of Norway. Thank you."

Don't thank *me*, Captain Ullebust. Thank *you* and your associate vikings who stayed awake all night and adjusted switches and pulled levers so that *I* would not fall into the Atlantic. Thank Messrs. Pratt and *Whitney* for causing those propellers to continue forming vague discs of gray in front of each motor. Thank *you*, Mr. Douglas and all *your* associates for holding together these several hundred thousand-odd bits of metal and wire and cloth, hour after hour, in the face of a three-hundred-mile gale and a burning sun and icy rains. Thank you all, but for *goodness'* sake, don't thank *me*.

And *tack för mat*, Anne-Lise.

ROUTE IN NORWAY

Norway

2

Oslo

THE CLOUDS ROLLED AWAY AS OUR PLANE COASTED earthward between spruce-green hills. We looked down into a broad valley dotted with red farm buildings, the surrounding fields ruled with strange vertical lines, which, we later discovered, were the ever-present Norwegian hay-drying racks.

We spotted the airport. The only thing that was missing from the picture was Oslo.

The plane slowed down on the concrete landing strip and then, to our surprise, turned off onto the grass and bounced nonchalantly across the fields in the direction of a long frame building. As George said, it was an undignified thing for a transatlantic plane to do. An ocean crossing should terminate in something more formal than a daisy patch.

Sara's new Plymouth Suburban had been sent over by boat weeks ahead. Elaborate arrangements had been made to have it meet us at the airport, partly because it satisfied our dramatic sense to step from the plane into our own car, and partly because we had read somewhere that taxis were hard to get at the Oslo airport.

The latter was one of the great gems of understatement. If any taxi had ever invaded this bucolic scene, its driver must have been on his way to retirement or escaping the police. As we descended the steps from the plane, the only vehicle in sight was an abandoned two-wheel cart under a nearby tree.

Inside the airport building, customs officials were engaged in the international process of inserting fingers along the inside edges of suitcases. A large bus rumbled up. I tried to telephone the Royal Norwegian Automobile Club about our car, but there are twenty-nine letters in the Norwegian alphabet and to a twenty-six-letter man who hasn't slept well, this is a great handicap. A kindly Norse stepped into the picture, and to my amazement I made connections with the right person immediately. Somehow or other it should have been more difficult.

The car, thought the voice on the other end of the phone, was on its way. It couldn't be sure, it only *thought* so. But if it *wasn't* on its way—I was disconnected and my Norwegian friend had left.

We watched the bus fill up. Would we go with it, or would we wait? We decided to wait. The bus rolled away down the narrow road, presumably in the direction of Oslo. The customs officials disappeared like characters in an Oriental fairy tale and were replaced by a number of cows which came out of a neighboring field and began to nibble the grass in front of the airport building. A midsummer stillness filled the air.

We were so sleepy that we only wanted to lie down under the tree and the two-wheel cart. That was all we asked of Norway at the moment. Then, with a self-conscious honking of its brand-new horn, Sara's green beauty came dashing around a bend in the road and drew up beside the airport building with a flourish that almost took the corner off the loading platform.

We have only one bit of advice for anyone making a transatlantic flight for the first time.

Write off the day of arrival.

Veteran transatlantic commuters will scoff at this. They will claim that they can step aboard a plane and sleep like so many babies until they touch the ground on the other side. They are either liars or we just did not have the stuff of which transatlantic commuters are made.

Our plane arrived in Oslo on Friday morning. We had been told that in midsummer everyone went to the country over the week end. As we had no desire to be marooned in a deserted city on Sunday, we decided, before leaving the United States, to mop up the sight-seeing situation on Friday and Saturday and move out for the west coast on Sunday morning.

It looked so easy on paper. We were scheduled to arrive at half-past nine in the morning. Surely we could go to the hotel, bathe, and be ready for anything by ten-thirty. I had a few letters of introduction to present. This I could do before lunch, while George, Lucy, and Sara eliminated museums, art galleries and other odds-and-ends.

Then we would lunch at Frognerseteren, up above the ski jump, overlooking the town. In the afternoon we would take in the Vigeland statues in the Frogner Park plus a few churches and in the evening, dine with friends at the Bristol.

What happened was so different.

We actually arrived at eight-thirty, an hour early, but by the time we reached the hotel and unpacked a few of the more creasable things, it was ten o'clock and, as far as our weary bodies were concerned, the day was over. There was a message waiting for us, however, instructing us to drop in at Bennett's Travel Bureau and pick up our accommodations—and there was an implication that we had better not fool around too long before doing so.

Calling on our last reserves we staggered over to Bennett's office on Karl Johansgate. There, in the midst of what seemed like hopeless confusion, we found the amazing Mr. Ottesen. He led us through a crowd of milling people to a tiny room at the end of a corridor where, without any confusion whatsoever, he handed us two neat little books containing coupons for our hotel rooms, baths, and breakfasts for the next fifty-four days and simultaneously relieved us of a staggering sum of money.

We were not used to paying for 216 nights' lodgings and breakfasts in this casual way. However, once we had recovered from the initial shock, it gave us the pleasant feeling that, somehow or other, the trip was free.

When we first began to study the road maps of Scandinavia, we had visualized ourselves as loafing along each day until we found some charming little country inn. There we would linger until the urge to move on stole over us.

Like so many other dreams, however, this one differed sharply from reality. Scandinavia suffers from a lack of hotels, charming or otherwise, with the result that rooms are booked far in advance even in the humble places; and getting into the great, haughty hostelries like the Bristol in Oslo, the Grand in Stockholm, and the d'Angleterre in Copenhagen, is a feat comparable only to obtaining tickets for a New York musical hit.

So we abandoned our gypsy instincts, pocketed our fat books of coupons and our deflated books of traveler's checks and found ourselves standing once more on Karl Johansgate.

It was a quarter of twelve. George mentioned the fact that we were falling a bit behind with sight-seeing plans. Lucy and Sara said that their only sight-seeing plan was to eat and go to bed. They did not care where they ate or what, as long as they could do it quickly and at a place less than a block away.

We lunched sleepily at Frascati's, looking down from the second-floor windows on the park and the endless flow of bicycles and the fresh, healthy-looking boys and girls in red sweaters and shorts, great knapsacks on their backs, waiting on the corner for buses.

Shortly after lunch we were in bed.

That evening, still groggy, we drove into the hills to the north

The ever-present rumble of white water is Norway's
aural trademark. (*Norwegian National Travel Office*)

Tan, close-coupled, crew-cut children of the fjords. (*Normanns Kunstforlag*)

Norwegian scenery never relaxes. (*Norwegian National Travel Office*)

Ancient warehouses on the river Nid. (*Norwegian National Travel Office*)

Headquarters of the Hanseatic League, Bergen. (*Eberh. B. Oppi*)

Give a Norwegian a bit of level ground and he will start a farm if he has to get to it by helicopter. (*Normanns Kunstforlag*)

Norwegian road engineers are born opti-
mists. (*Norwegian National Travel Office*)

Long rows of drying hay strip the mountain valleys

Where man gives over to the goats and trolls. (*Harstad Forlag*)

At Stalheim the uplands descend to sea level in a
single bound. (*Norwegian National Travel Office*)

Kvikne—Balholm—call it which you will, such a setting
needs no help from names. (*Scandinavian Airlines Photo*)

Ancient Norwegian stave church. Christian? Yes, but why alienate the old gods unnecessarily. (*Swedish Travel Information Bureau*)

St. Olav's Cathedral and Olav Trygvasson's statue dominate Trondheim just as the two Olavs have dominated the life of its citizens for almost ten centuries. (*Mittet & Co.*)

of the city, past the ski jump at Holmenkollen to the rambling log restaurant at Frognerseteren where we ate on the deep porch and looked down on the Oslofjord dotted with islands and white sails. It was half-past eight, but this was July 14 and it would be light until midnight. The fjord was bathed in the level rays of the evening sun and the red roofs of the summer cottages along its wooded shores glowed like wild flowers against the blue-black of the evergreens.

We finished our first fish dinner, descended to water level and hurried to bed.

With scarcely a pause for breath, the northern sun was back on the job, forcing its way into our bedrooms through the chinks in the heavy, red curtains and flooding all with brightness.

Someone had given us black sleeping masks as a going-away present. We had mistakenly placed them in the same category as ear-stoppers and anti-snore nose-pins and almost left them behind. Now, as this subarctic klieg light pried my lids apart, I observed a masked bandit sleeping peacefully in the next bed. It was probably Lucy, but the momentary uncertainty made me feel like a character in an international spy novel.

In the United States one would have tucked his head under the bedclothes. In Norway and Denmark, however, there are no bedclothes. We were having our first experience with *dyner*, those extraordinary masses of feathers under which the Norwegians and Danes love to crawl each night.

For the benefit of those who lead sheltered lives let me explain that a *dyne* is a kind of a gigantic pillowcase, tailored to the size of the mattress beneath it and stuffed with something which is a cross between a comforter and a huge pillow. Quite obviously such an object is untuckable. It covers the body as long as the body behaves itself, but it has no patience with restlessness. Let the

17

hands or feet twitch ever so slightly and out they go into the darkness.

There are undoubtedly many people who enjoy having their hands and feet popping into the night, but for those conditioned in early life to being tucked snugly into cribs like larvae in a cocoon, such unaccustomed freedom merely breeds insecurity.

Life *beneath* the *dyne* also presents its problems. To live comfortably under one of them, regardless of the outside temperature, would require thermostatic body control. Perhaps the Scandinavians have it. The only way that we could cope with the situation, however, was to lie under them until we were soaked with sweat and then throw them on the floor until we began to shake with cold.

Turning over in bed also presents major problems, for the *dyne*, being a one-piece job, moves with the body. If you do not quite understand what this means, inflate an air mattress and try rolling around under it.

A broad-shouldered man, turning from his right to his left side, should be able to give his *dyne* the old heave-ho to the floor without its touching the edge of the bed. Less athletically built men merely push it half off their bodies, leaving the front side smothered and the back side exposed to the chill of the night. This is the stuff that schizophrenics are made of.

But enough of *dyner*. We have already given them disproportionate space. It is barely possible, however, that these are the really important things—the things from which nostalgia is created. May we not find that in the years to come, when a foot escapes from a carelessly tucked sheet, a flood of memories of shadowed fjords and sod-roofed houses, of hairpin turns and waterfalls and bicycles and all the other loveliness of Scandinavia will unreel themselves across our sleepy brains?

In spite of the fact that we had just spent our first night under a *dyne*, the world looked like our oyster on Saturday morning and the problem of mopping up Oslo in one day presented no difficulties whatsoever.

That was before we saw our first Folkemuseum. The Scandinavians have a passion for collecting ancient buildings. Show a Norwegian, Swede or Dane a house over five hundred years old and, with antlike patience, he will drag it hundreds of miles over hill and dale to his local municipal park, where he will add it to a neat little synthetic village whose newest house was weatherbeaten when Columbus discovered America.

The Oslo Folkemuseum is not one village but many, scattered through a great park, and it was there that we had our first experience with early Norwegian doorways. In the rugged days of old, visitors were not necessarily friendly and as a matter of prudence it was safer if people did not come rushing pell-mell into the living room. To discourage this the door lintels were set low enough to catch the impetuous entrant between the bridge of his nose and his hairline, and the thresholds were raised three to six inches above the floor so that the visitor, half-stunned by the one, would trip over the other and enter the room in no position or condition to put up an argument.

It was an interesting historical lesson which we learned the hard way. To ram one's head into an oak beam is a painful experience at best, but, unless concussion results, the effects should pass away in an hour or so. To continue ramming the cranium into hardwood lintels every five minutes over a period of two hours, however, is discouraging if not permanently deranging.

But before we had finished with the Oslo Folkemuseum we had gained a momentum which was not to be stopped by a few lintels; and before the day was over we had galloped through the viking ship museum, popped in and out of innumerable churches, gaped at the new Town Hall and finally, late in the afternoon, dragged our burning feet through Frogner Park, which contains what is locally referred to as the Vigeland Layout.

Gustav Vigeland was a sculptor with elephantiasis of the thyroid gland. In 1906 he conceived a fountain for the city of Oslo. It was a fountain to end fountains, calling for half the amount of water each day that the city was then using for more practical purposes. The water department did not worry much, because the fountain also called for so many stone groups that no one believed Vigeland would ever live to finish them.

He did—and acquired such an impetus in the process that the city was in a constant turmoil finding room for his work. The problem was only solved when a great park was turned over to him. That would undoubtedly have been inadequate had he not died in 1943.

Whether Vigeland was crazy or great is a controversy that can be called upon to fill a gap in any Norwegian conversation. Certainly, he made stone live, although he caused it to assume rather odd forms of life.

Vigeland may be said to have glorified the naked human from the cradle to the grave. In fact, he went further than that and produced what is perhaps the first and only statue of a foetus standing on its head. You get the impression that he may have been frequently exasperated with his fellow men, but never bored with life.

We liked Oslo, but it was an insult to a fair city to attempt acquaintance in two days—one of which had been largely spent in bed.

3

Geilo

WE STOWED THE BAGGAGE IN THE REAR OF THE CAR AND headed for the west coast of Norway, feeling as the boys on the "Kontiki" must have felt when the Peruvian naval tug set them adrift on the eastern edge of the Pacific.

Great featherbed clouds floated majestically above us like an aerial escort as we drove somewhat nervously out of Oslo, a dark green chip on a river of bicycles. It was a colorful stream made up of all age groups—blond young gods and goddesses, riding knee to knee, dressed in every conceivable costume and lack of costume; parental Norsemen (and women) pedaling unperturbed through the traffic, their offspring strapped into tiny seats on the handle bars or behind the saddles—or both; octogenarians, gliding sedately along in the effortless manner with which all Scandinavians ride bicycles, regardless of age.

It was a vivid scene, but one which we would have preferred to watch from the side of the road rather than from a car which we were attempting to push through the melee. From where we sat, there was something suicidal about the whole thing. Each time another car passed us, going in the opposite direction, we were forced deeper into the living stream until we seemed to be literally shoving cyclists out of the way with our fenders.

Fortunately, however, Scandinavians have a fluid quality which enables them to flow unconcernedly around dangerous objects. Had any one of us found ourselves on a bicycle instead of in the car, we would have ditched ourselves immediately and started walking. But these amazing people rode placidly on their way, ignoring the fact that their knees almost brushed the car each time their feet rose on the pedals. With a two-inch-wobble leeway between them and disaster, they leaned forward and nuzzled their young with soft sounds of love, or they half-turned in their saddles and smiled gaily at the little Norsemen in the rear. The only thing they didn't do was wobble.

Strapped neatly to racks over the rear wheels were great packs, and a knapsack bulged between the shoulder blades of almost every rider. How they could pump those loads uphill was more than we could understand. Norwegian legs, however, are apparently built of steel, for they not only rode uphill, but they didn't even lean forward while doing it. Never once did we see a Norwegian, a Swede or a Dane sink to the level of standing on his pedals, American fashion.

Gradually we drew away from this mass migration. The valleys became narrower, the mountains bigger. The pine forests covered the land with a blue-green blanket.

We ate our first picnic lunch on the shores of a long narrow lake in the Hallingdal. In Norway *dal* means valley. Across the deep blue waters of the lake, billows of low, purple mountains rolled away into the distance. Patches of white snow lay on their sides and tops.

Our road had been skirting the base of a mountain which cascaded into the lake in the precipitate manner of all Norwegian landscapes. Several hundred feet up on its sharply sloping sides, an ambitious engineer had hacked out a shelf wide enough for a railroad track. Occasionally, a toy train would pop out of a tunnel with a thin hoot, scuttle along the narrow ledge and disappear into another tunnel. One had the feeling that it was running on a circular track.

A mountain stream came roaring down the slope, dived under the road above us, and took a final plunge through a rocky chute to mingle with the more sedate waters of the lake. On a narrow beach, two buckskin Norwegian ponies with crew-cut manes switched their tails thoughtfully.

The hotel had furnished us with a Norwegian picnic lunch. We had not yet learned to carry our ingredients and roll our own. In the boxes was an incredible assortment of open sandwiches, great slabs of smoked salmon which, when we bit into them, pulled off the bread and hung on our chins like lolling tongues, moist red ham, sliced pork and hard-boiled eggs, without salt. We had an empty milk bottle in the car which we filled at the stream and washed down our meal with cold glacier water which George declared was the cause of goiter among the Himalayans.

As the day wore on, the roads began to narrow to a point where we frequently had to stop before passing another car. There was white water in sight most of the time and its sound never left us.

It was a country of farm buildings with vertical clapboards, log houses, and brilliant orange-red barns—a country of mountains and farm-studded valleys, rushing streams which broadened momentarily until they achieved the dignity of rivers and then went back to rushing again. George said it reminded him of the White Mountains, which annoyed Sara and Lucy profoundly, for they regarded any comparison with familiar things as a cynical attempt to destroy romance.

We spent the night at the Holms Høyfjellshotel. It stands on a hillside above the village of Geilo which, as nearly as we could make out, is pronounced Yale-o. But that is not vital. For no matter how one pronounces a Scandinavian name, the Scandinavians will pronounce it differently.

From our bedroom windows we looked down on the red-tiled

roofs of a toy village scattered among the trees. A white church, protruding through the foliage, watched over it like a benign shepherd. Still further down, at the bottom of the narrow valley, we had a glimpse of the ever-present white, tumbling water. Its muted roar was in our ears all night.

That evening we met a Norwegian industrialist who joined us after dinner for coffee and brandy. He discussed many things of world importance in such rapid English that it was hard to follow him. A pale young man entered the room, bowed, and sat down before a grand piano.

He could play, this young man. As the music increased in volume, the industrialist was obliged to raise his voice to a shout, which he did without hesitation. The young man went up a notch. The industrialist pulled out all his stops. It was a competition between oratory and the arts—a contest somewhat embarrassing to us as it was plain that the public was on the side of the arts.

Finally, the young man stopped in a burst of crashing chords which left the industrialist yelling into the momentary silence which followed. He was a man not easily thrown off balance, however. Cupping his hands he raised them above his head and clapped madly. "Bravo," he shouted, "brilliant! A magnificent performance!"

It was at Dr. Holms's Hotel that we had our first experience with a Norwegian *koldtbord* breakfast. In the center of the dining room stood a great table at least fifteen feet long, its snowy cloth hidden by laden platters and bowls. Sara has a strong statistical streak in her otherwise feminine nature. She went out to the front office and returned with one of the attractive blondes who presided behind the desk, from whom she requested a detailed inventory of this extraordinary layout. Sara's notes will give a vague idea of the situation.

Fruit department	*Tyttebær.* Our informant said that the English called these cowberries, which was all right with us, but did not help much.
	Orange marmalade—in great bowls.
	Apple marmalade—ditto.
Cereal department	Rice Krispies!!
Fish department	Herring in oil.
	Pickled herring.
	What she described as "another kind of herring."
	What she described as "another kind of herring."
	Herring salad. All the above mixed with carrots and what-have-you. The whole well tossed.
	Sursild—which she described as "another kind of herring salad."
	Sardines.
	Fish pudding—square, cold, sliced. Looked like French toast, but tasted quite different.
	Fish cakes.
	Redfish salad.
Meat department	Pork sausages.
	Wiener schnitzel.
	Liver loaf.
	Sylte—cold, sliced. She was very reticent about *sylte.* All she was prepared to say for quotation was that it came from a pig.
	Ham.
	Salami.
	Chops. This is our interpretation. She merely shrugged her shoulders.
Cheese department	There were four Gargantuan cheeses. Three she said were made from cow's milk

25

	and one from goat's milk. She called them *Roquefort-ost, guadaost, gjetost* and *gammelost*. Why she did so she would not tell us.
Pickle department	All 57 varieties.
	Pickled beets.
Bread department	We counted 15 different kinds ranging from hard rolls to sweet wafers and including Norwegian *flatbrød*. At that point we were pushed away by hungry guests.
Salad department	Great bowls of lettuce and tomato salad.

Our guide was obviously touched by our interest.

"Ah," she said, "you should see it in winter. Then we have the skiers who bring appetites. We have a larger table. It is truly beautiful. People take colored pictures of it."

We picked up plates from a three-foot stack at the end of the table and walked slowly round and round this extraordinary exhibit, like visitors at a country fair. The other guests did likewise. Occasionally one of them would drop out of line, spear a tidbit, and then resume his slow march. To people brought up on the disciplined frugality of orange juice, eggs, coffee and toast, early-morning decisions of this sort are confusing.

Almost all *koldtbord* novices fall into two groups. Those in the first wish to establish themselves as citizens of the world and take a little of everything—with special emphasis on the unidentifiable dishes or those most calculated to revolt their less sophisticated companions.

Those in the second group decide that all they want in the world is a glass of orange juice and some hot, buttered toast, neither of which can be had. They then work themselves into a tantrum and are apt to be unapproachable for at least an hour.

Once you are seated at the table, polite young boys approach, bearing bowls of boiled eggs and big pots of strong coffee. Regardless of what else you may eat for breakfast in Scandinavia, a single boiled egg is a national requirement. The word single should be emphasized. The guest is only supposed to take one, which he up-ends in a tiny eggcup and eats from the shell.

George caused us to lose caste wherever we went by seizing a double handful of eggs and breaking them with ostentatious violence into his coffee cup (before it had been filled with coffee, of course). Lucy once commented that it must have been a man like George who originated the phrase "a clutch of eggs."

The egg boys were obviously shocked but always courteous. In fact, we never saw a more Chesterfieldian group than these Norwegian egg boys. On our first morning in Geilo, I observed two of them collide between tables. Instead of the usual coarse dialogue which would have followed such a meeting at home, they disengaged, bowed, murmured some smiling phrases and went their ways.

It was raining—our first taste of Norwegian west-coast weather. There is something undesirable about loading baggage into a car in the rain. Some overeager co-operator always puts one bag in wrong and eventually the whole mass has to be pulled out into the downpour and a fresh start made.

In a field beside the hotel a group of men and women, seemingly oblivious of the weather, were engaged in their incessant midsummer task of hanging wisps of hay over wires stretched one above the other between poles planted in the ground.

All through Norway these "fences" of hay stripe the fields; in the valleys, on the slopes, on inaccessible patches of land high up on the mountainsides. Not a square foot of soil capable of growing precious grass is overlooked. Men and women work with hand scythes between the boulders beside the streams, between the roots of trees, on embankments so steep that they must hold on with one hand and cut with the other.

It was at the Holms Hotel that we began our education in the life and habits of Scandinavian porters. They are called porters, but that is a totally inadequate word, for they are far more than luggage toters—they are, in fact, the very lifeblood of the hotel which they serve and no Scandinavian hotel can be better than its porter.

It is in the country places like Geilo that they reach their peaks of greatness. There they act as room clerks, baggage carriers, cashiers, bellhops, information centers, trip arrangers, switchboard operators, and, in their spare moments, sell postage stamps which they insist upon licking and applying to the never-ending stream of postal cards and mail which is funished them by the guests.

This act seems to be a basic item in the Scandinavian porter's code. Never once, in the great hotels or the humble, did one of them permit us to lick or apply our own postage stamps. It interested us to calculate the quantity of glue which passed through the system of a good porter in a single busy season. They were fine, strapping specimens in spite of it, however, and Lucy had a theory that possibly the glue furnished them the vitamins which they would otherwise have lacked because of the absence of orange juice.

In the United States we have been spoiled by the smooth efficiency of our modern hotels. When, for example, we step up to the cashier's window after breakfast, we have learned to expect, as an inherent right of citizenship, that a dour-faced woman will push our bill under the grillwork without an instant's delay. Actually this mechanical approach has taken much of the adventure out of hotel bills and tended to commercialize them. In Scandinavia they retain many of the old sporting customs, however, and while it may take more time to find out what you owe, there is ample compensation in watching a good hotel porter approach his work.

All the guests who are leaving immediately after breakfast assemble around the desk as soon as they have swallowed the last herring, and demand their bills. They give the porter excellent reasons why they should have special attention. They must go all the way to Oslo that day, their bags are all in the car and they are ready to start, their wife is not well, their little boy won't stand still, etc., etc. The porter nods sympathetically, but pays no attention to them.

He opens a drawer and takes out a double handful of slips. These bits of paper he proceeds to sort like a solitaire player. A lady approaches with a batch of postcards which she has just selected from the racks. She assures the porter that he does not need to count them. There are eleven. He nods agreement, drops all work on the slips, and counts the cards carefully, finding twelve. She wants stamps. He takes a key from his pocket, unlocks a drawer, counts out the stamps, makes change, locks the drawer, replaces the key in his pocket, licks each stamp and places it squarely and neatly where indicated on the card. Then he throws the cards into a box with the accuracy of a basketball player and resumes his solitaire game with the little white slips.

At this point in an American hotel physical violence would raise its ugly head, but there is something so imperturbable about a Scandinavian porter that the mob spirit never has a chance to gain momentum. One would as soon try to push a glacier around or tell Jupiter to step on it. Everyone stands pressed against the desk and stares at the slips hypnotically.

A woman comes up with a twenty-dollar traveler's check. The porter drops the slips, unlocks a cashbox, makes the exchange, locks the cashbox, returns it to its place under the desk, and resumes play.

A man pushes through the crowd and asks when the ferries run between Kinsarvik and Kvanndal. The porter takes down a volume

as big as a New York telephone book and after considerable thumb-
wetting, gives the required information. The man thanks him
and says he was just wondering. The porter returns the book and
continues making out bills.

Strangely enough, your bill is placed in your hands much more
quickly than you would have thought possible—if you had thought
it possible at all. To visitors from the United States, Scandinavian
bills are worth waiting for. Trained as we are to expect highway
robbery and extortion as part of the price of existence, these bills are
a source of joy and pleasure.

We gave up our room, bath and breakfast coupons, paid for
the extras, wrung the porter's hand hysterically and went out to
the waiting car.

4

Hardangerfjord

WITHOUT SENSING IT, WE HAD BEEN CLIMBING STEADILY since leaving Oslo. When we pulled away from Geilo in the driving rain we were twenty-six hundred feet above sea level and the grade was growing steeper.

We were leaving the fertile valleys and working up to a great lonely plateau, to a world of rain and snow and low-hanging clouds, a world of reindeer moss and gray, outcropping rocks and desolation. We passed an island-dotted lake. On the opposite side, snow-covered mountains hid their tops in the mist. Beside the road, the red houses of a little village huddled together for protection against the surrounding loneliness. A profusion of grass and flowers sprouted from their sod roofs, giving the only touch of color to the gray scene.

At Haugastol even the railroad abandoned us and we were on our own, a very small green car in a very big gray place. The timber line was below us and there was nothing here but reindeer moss, rock, snow, and water. Water poured down from the thawing snowfields above us, rushing between the rocks and cutting foaming channels through the moss, pausing a moment to consolidate its energy in sinister black ponds, then dashing on in its reckless plunge toward the sea.

We were on the Hardangervidda, crossing it on the famous Reindeer Road which is open for travel for only a brief period each year. Here, according to the books, is the habitat of the largest wild reindeer herds in the world and, from the looks of the place, it is also the home ground of all trolls. We watched carefully, but saw neither.

Long, wooden snowsheds made tunnels over the road in improbable places. We stopped at the entrance to one of them and explored its gloomy interior. It would have been no surprise to have turned up a few odd bodies. Nearby stood the loneliest house in the world. I walked over to it, stepping gingerly on the mounds of reindeer moss, in order not to break through into the ooze and mud which lies just below the soft crust.

A blind slapped in a sudden gust. The door was hooked. I unlatched it and pushed it open without enthusiasm, fully expecting to find the aftermath of an ax murder. But the bleak little room merely contained an innocent litter of newspapers, cans, bits of firewood, and the flotsam of unloving tenants.

Over an untidy pile of stove wood in one corner someone had written: "Anna and Nils." It seemed like a rather uniform world. I closed the door, hooked it carefully, and picked my way back to the Plymouth feeling that the hound of the Baskervilles was already sniffing my tracks.

We reached the edge of the plateau, where the land plunges almost straight down to sea level, and turned off for lunch at Fossli, a little inn which stands at the point where the river Bjoreia takes a running leap over a pile of rocks and lands in a heap five hundred feet below.

The Norwegians are not sissies about such places. They do not spoil them trying to protect fools against themselves with handrails and signs warning them to keep away from the edge. There is the edge. Keep away from it, go up to it or fall over it if you wish. Use it as you are accustomed to using edges.

We approached this particular one on hands and knees and finally lay on the flat rock to look straight down along the white column of living water to the point where it struck the rocks almost a tenth of a mile down and bounced back in an arc of angry spray.

Having recovered from the impact and gathered itself together again, the Bjoreia went roaring toward the fjord through a narrow canyon. From where we lay we could see the corkscrew road which optimistic Norwegian engineers had blasted out of the headwall. At the bottom of the gorge it joined the river and romped along beside it until road and river disappeared around a protruding cliff.

We left Fossli and dropped over the rim. It was our first headwall road and they never failed to be exciting. We always felt sorry for people who must see this country from boats and trains and planes, for it is necessary to become a pinpoint on the face of a gigantic rock mass to sense the immensity and grandeur of this land—as well as one's own insignificance.

Mention has already been made of George's tremendous powers of association. He had traveled everywhere and his mind had all the chain reactions of an atomic pile. Now, as we negotiated our first hairpin turn somewhat overcautiously, he was suddenly reminded of a donkey trip he had once taken in the high Andes. He apparently had not thought of the matter for years, as a result of which the whole thing had been rather dammed up inside him. As he warmed to the subject, the words began to tumble out like the waters of the river below.

Once in the groove, George hated to be interrupted. He was an artist who demanded undivided attention. But Lucy and Sara had little respect for taletellers. "Look! Look at that!" one or the other of them would scream. George would glare, but there was nothing to be done. He was up against two of the world's most ruthless interrupters.

The road and the river competed for a foothold in the narrow canyon. Occasionally the river would win and drive the road into

33

a long tunnel with rocky windows cut in its side, through which we could see the untiring water tumbling over itself a few feet below.

We came to the Hardangerfjord at the end of one of its main arms—the Eidfjord. It was all so like the travel pictures that it was hard to keep in mind which was real and which reproduction. Gray-green mountains rose straight from the still water and at the extreme end of the fjord a little town huddled in their shadow. The eye wandered over the water, unconsciously looking for the white cruise-liner which traditionally should be lying just off-shore.

The Ullensvang Hotel is a long, yellow two-story building, sitting placidly by the water's edge. Its spacious halls carry the faint aroma of generations of herring. It is an odor which would enable an experienced traveler to identify a Norwegian country hotel blindfolded, but one which never offends. It is a mark of authenticity which the guest seeks on entering, just as a buyer sniffs the genuineness of tweed.

The second-floor rooms, on the fjord side, have balconies where one may sit and drowse and watch the play of light on the mountains which rise from the water's edge on the opposite shore, a mile or more away. Their tops are capped with patches of snow from which the water trickles off in a dozen rivulets in the manner of all water trickling from ice cakes on a warm day. The only difference is that each of these rivulets contains enough power to light a small city and their faint rumble forms a background for all other sounds.

To the south, a glacier had crept to the edge of the mountain where it hung over the water indecisively as if measuring the distance before taking the plunge. An occasional gull flapped and coasted its way down the middle of the fjord. From the dark shadow of the further shore came the put-put of a fishing boat. Two children were calling down in the village. A wisp of cloud got caught on the peak of the mountain opposite.

Johan was the porter at the Ullensvang Hotel. He beamed at us through the window of the Plymouth as we came to a stop. Johan looked about eighteen. He was tall and thin with an Oxford accent, and an uncontrollable lock of hair which was always in his eyes.

Country hotels in Norway have no elevators. Our rooms were on the third floor. In the United States Johan would have been called out immediately by the hotel porter's union until the management had provided some method of reaching the top floor other than by walking. But he was a Norwegian, raised in a country where it is as normal to go up as it is to go forward.

He was such a fragile-looking lad that I would gladly have handed him my brief case and coped with the bags myself. He pushed me gently aside, however, and placed a heavy suitcase under either arm; then he bent his knees slightly and picked up another suitcase in each hand. Just as I was about to protest, he squatted for the second time. I thought his knees were buckling. On the contrary, he had, in some mysterious manner, hooked onto two additional pieces of baggage with his middle fingers.

"Come," he said, smiling pleasantly, "I will show you to your rooms."

We followed him up three flights of broad stairs. Norwegian hotel stairs must be broad to permit the passage of human baggage racks like Johan. "Do you do this many times a day?" I asked.

"Ah yes," he answered cheerfully, as if I had stumbled on a pleasant truth.

"You must get pretty tired."

"Ah no," he said, "the hotel has only three stories—and also I do many other things."

He did. He registered us. He took care of the telephone switchboard. He sold postcards and stamps (asserting, of course, his licking privilege). He gave information. He planned trips. He helped out in the dining room. And before we left, he washed the Plymouth.

The Ullensvang breakfast layout competed favorably with that of Geilo for sheer lavishness, but we were beginning to learn what to avoid.

There was a small fish about four inches long which must be dear to the heart of Norwegians, for we met it everywhere. Its principal features were a pair of overgrown and mawkishly sentimental eyes—eyes which were a cross between those of Eddie Cantor and a wounded antelope.

To anyone who dislikes emotion in the morning, such eyes could become most distasteful. They looked up at one reproachfully and seemed to be saying, "I once had a mother, also." Of course, when lying on a plate, only one eye could reproach at a time, but when you could not stand it any longer and turned the thing over, there was the other eye, beaming the same message.

That was one dish we gave up.

Then there were bowls filled with sliced tomatoes. Hanging to their rims by a few of their many spidery legs were dozens of little pink crayfish, or *kreps*, staring with beady, black eyes at the ceiling.

We avoided them also.

And then there was a certain kind of goat cheese which tasted much the way a goat smells.

We discontinued using that.

Lest anyone misunderstand, however, this is merely an expression of our personal tastes. Many undoubtedly found these dishes pleasing and the remaining forty-seven selections met with our unqualified approval.

Johan had arranged a boat trip for us. A friend of his had a very fine pleasure boat. We watched it coming across from the opposite shore and saw it stop in the middle of the fjord. Johan, who had come down to the shore to observe, assured us that this was not his friend's fault. The stoppage must be blamed, he felt, on the motor, which had undoubtedly gone dead.

The friend arrived eventually, a youth of savage beauty. His yellow hair rippled back from his forehead like a curly mane. His great chest was sparsely covered with a torn, buttonless shirt. He seemed to fill the boat with his bulk.

We huddled in the bow, separated from the blond giant by an odd-looking engine resembling an outsize kerosene stove. Johan, on the stone dock, pushed us off gaily, waving good-by. The breeze caught the boat and nosed us rapidly away from the shore. We explained to our skipper that we would like to run up the fjord toward Odda for an hour and then return.

It took us some time to realize that he did not speak or understand a word of English. He paid no more attention to us than to the mewing of two gulls who soared and swooped hopefully overhead. From under a seat he produced a blowtorch which he proceeded to pump up and light. When it was roaring satisfactorily he inserted the nozzle into a hole in the engine and held it there until the surrounding area became cherry-pink.

By this time the Ullensvang Hotel was a yellow speck in the distance. The gulls had grown weary and returned to their stations just outside the kitchen. The skipper extinguished the torch and inserted a crank handle into the flywheel. There was a dreadful roar which almost caused us to abandon ship. The young man seemed quite unperturbed. From under a tangle of rope he produced an oversized monkey wrench and proceeded to bring the engine under control by taking a turn on a huge nut.

It was just as well, perhaps, that he did not speak English. If he had, we might not have seen Agatunet, which is a little Folkemuseum hidden away in an equally small village and clinging miraculously to the side of a mountain.

As soon as we gained headway, he headed our bow toward the opposite shore and eventually pulled up beside an old dock. He pointed upward and then stretched himself out on the sun-baked planks and was asleep before we had started to climb.

A cart track wound its way up the hill in a series of traverses leading through flowering orchards. A woman, seated on the lower step of a house, saw us coming and called through the open door behind her. An old man came out and as we approached he offered to show us about, with an accent which seemed strangely out of place in these surroundings.

We asked him where he had learned to speak English so well. He said he had picked it up in North Dakota between 1906 and 1926. The place became too congested for him, however, so he returned to his home village and now, if we would be so good, he would show us the house that was eight hundred years old.

Eventually, we staggered back down the path, our heads reeling with pain from the impact of a dozen five-foot door lintels. Perhaps the early Norsemen wore their bronze war helmets in the house.

Our boatman roused himself with difficulty from deep sleep. We indicated with watch and gesture that we wanted to go up the fjord toward the glacier for half an hour. He nodded, lit the blowtorch and ran us back to the hotel without further argument.

Behind the Ullensvang and the village of Lofthus rises what I believe geographers call a cirque. The ever-present mountains which dominate both shores of the fjord, recede at this point into a colossal amphitheater whose vertical walls tower a thousand feet above the handkerchief farms which take advantage of every inch of arable land in the arena.

Its upper rim is marked with white by the snowfields. Three great falls hurl themselves down the cliff face and hit the bottom with a rumble that fills the village below with constant sound.

A wagon road climbed up from the fjord through acres of cherry orchards where men and women stood on ladders working as only people do in a country where but three per cent of the surface of the land is good for farming.

Then we were above the orchards and the farmhouses, in rocky pasture land splashed with great daubs of purple foxglove. Through it the merged waters of the falls roared in panic toward the fjord as if a thousand trolls pursued them. Eventually the pastures merged into first-growth timber and the whole scene took on the look of a steel engraving in an old copy of Goethe's poems.

Two girls passed driving cows. In almost any other country in the world, one would not have expected much from girls carrying out such a humble errand in a lonely place like this, but in Norway the girls manage, somehow or other, to look like models for colored postal cards whether they are driving cows up lonely cirques or hanging up wisps of hay in the rain. When George took their picture they giggled, indicating that they were human as well as picturesque.

It was getting chilly. We retraced our steps. A lone cow emerged from the woods and followed us, lowing as if its heart was broken. Occasionally, it closed in on us and pushed us from behind with its head. Sara, who prides herself on her command of animals, stamped her feet and ordered it home, but it was either homeless or did not understand English.

Lucy, who doesn't care much for animals, but who is, in many ways, more practical in her dealings with them, threw a rock at it. That seemed to register. The cow stopped and watched us sullenly as we descended the slope. We hoped that we were about to see the last of the friendless beast when suddenly it emitted a colossal burp and charged down the path after us. We threw ourselves behind bushes as it thundered past, its udder swinging like a tocsin bell. We lost sight of it around a turn, but we could follow its course down the valley by the clatter of loose stones. It probably disappeared eventually into the fjord. In the old days that would have been good for a legend.

Lowering, gray clouds hung over the mountains across the fjord, with touches of deep blue sky between them. The sun, flashing momentarily through the cloud masses, lit up the headwall behind us and threw a rainbow across its base. A rain squall was working its way down the fjord.

We found an empty table on the terrace of the hotel and ordered chilled sherry which, in this land of scarce spirit licenses, takes the place of the evening cocktail for the weary traveler. It is served in great beakers and a couple of them go a long way.

5

Bergen

WE HAD OUR FIRST EXPERIENCE WITH A NORWEGIAN CAR
ferry shortly after leaving Lofthus on our road to Bergen.

Back in the United States we had been assured that Norwegian
fjord ferries ran very frequently and that there was never any lack
of room. We found that they ran very infrequently and that there
was never any room at all. Fortunately Johan had, as usual, taken
matters into his capable hands and made a reservation for our car
on the ferry from Kinsarvik, a few miles north of Lofthus, which
would eventually set us down at Kvanndal on the north shore of the
Hardangerfjord.

Although the Kinsarvik ferry was built along the sound, traditional lines established for ferryboats years ago by New York harbor,
it was no lumbering, hacked-up affair designed for the pounding of
overland trailer trucks, but a neat little junior model built for
Austins and Sunbeams and Volvos. If a ferryboat can be jaunty this
one was as it lay at its dock, its fresh paint sparkling in the morning
sun.

The open place around the landing was already jammed with
waiting cars parked without any apparent order. The sight immediately increased our blood pressure by fifty points and brought us
out fighting. We had made reservations. No one was going to keep
us off that boat. We would protest this thing all the way up to the
Royal Palace.

A pleasant-looking man with a handful of papers approached.
"Good morning," he said, "you are Number Six. We are expecting

you. Please place this number on your windshield. You will be called." He handed us a cardboard disc containing our number, backed away a few feet and bowed.

I sprang from the car in astonishment and returned his bow. "Thank you," he said. "*Takk,*" I said in faultless Norwegian. "*Tusen takk.*"

Eventually the gaily striped pole barring the entrance to the ferry was lifted. In spite of all assurances we tensed ourselves for action, engine accelerated and in gear, ready for the rat race that experience had taught us was bound to follow in spite of our polite friend. Not a car moved.

From the crowd around the gangway someone called a number in Norwegian. A car in the rear of the group disentangled itself, did a dignified slalom through its parked neighbors, and drove aboard. Our friend approached, unhurried and urbane. "Number Six," he said, removing our tag, "and a pleasant journey."

"*Tusen takk,*" we shouted, and, in the interests of efficiency, resisted the impulse to get out and bow.

The road to Bergen winds over the tangled mountain ranges of the west coast, now skirting the shores of the Hardangerfjord, then dashing up a narrow valley and over a headwall where white water thunders all about.

We ate lunch on a rocky shelf at a point where a mountain stream took an enormous leap into space and fell into a pocket valley hundreds of feet below, disintegrating in the fall and coming neatly together again at the bottom to rush past a group of toy farm buildings and disappear into another gorge.

In the United States it would have been a Famous Spot, visited by thousands each year. There would have been places where one could buy banners and paperweights, decorated with colored pictures of the falls, and small birchbark canoes for the loved ones left behind and colored postals of brown bear with young. There would have been a hot-dog stand and a parking turnout, where for ten cents one could look through a pair of field glasses on a tripod, and green-tiled facilities and crumpled paper cups and all the other modern appurtenances that go with Famous Spots.

In this extraordinary country, however, our picnic place did not even have a name. One could park wherever the spirit moved and the only human being we saw was an unexplained woman who appeared suddenly on the road above us as we were finishing our lunch and began pacing nervously up and down.

It was such an unlikely place for nervous pacing by lone women that we concluded she might be waiting for us to go in order to do a Lover's Leap. So we obligingly eliminated our noon siesta, packed up the remnants of the lunch and left her in possession of the landscape to use it as she pleased.

Bergen is a beautiful old city lying at the mouth of the Hardangerfjord which, after the manner of Norwegian fjords, is called something else at this point. It is hemmed in against the sea by purple-gray mountains which, in the early days, isolated it from the land-world to the east and forced it to turn to the sea for its livelihood.

It acquired, in consequence, a cosmopolitan flavor which is still noticeable even in these days of standardized cosmopolitanism. It paid for its sophistication with a history of violence and bloodshed —a history that belies its name, which is derived from the Norwegian word *bjorgvin*, meaning pasture-amid-mountains.

There were, however, no remaining evidences of either violence or goriness as we drove through its broad streets late that afternoon. Nothing could have been more peaceful-looking than the cream-colored, Victorian exterior of the Hotel Norge or the gaffers who sunned themselves on the benches which flanked the entrance.

The hotel looked sleepily out over Ole Bulls Plass, a charming little park at the head of which sat Ole Bull himself. He had laid his famous violin at his feet and at the moment was good-naturedly allowing his head to be used as a landing field by a flock of starlings.

We like everything about the Norge; its broad corridors and huge, high-ceilinged bedrooms and the tiny balconies outside our windows where one could stand and look down on Ole Bull and the activities of his Plass. We liked everything about it in fact, but the doorsills which, in good Norwegian tradition, were four inches high causing us to fall in and out of our rooms in an undignified manner.

Immediately on arrival, George drafted me for a visit to the railroad station, for railroads are one of his many hobbies. If they all started from stations like the one in Bergen, I would have become an addict myself.

It was a gray stone building with a balcony running across its front which literally dripped with bright-colored flowers. Inside, iron baskets filled with flowers were suspended by chains from the lofty ceiling. On the platforms baskets of flowers hung between the posts. To the left of the tracks a tree-bordered lagoon supported a family of aimlessly circling ducks and, surrounding the yard on all sides, were the ever-present mountains. Not a bad beginning for a railroad.

It was ten o'clock before we finished dinner. Afterward, in the half light of a midsummer Norwegian evening, we walked through the narrow, winding streets of the old town where everything was incredibly small and unbelievably ancient. Soft lights filtered through the windows and superimposed shadow designs on the horseshoe pattern of the cobblestones, and in every window were flowers—flowers in pots, flowers in boxes, flowers in vases. In Norway, no one is too poor to have flowers or too tired, apparently, to care for them.

Perhaps the best-known landmark in Bergen is the famous row of warehouses once occupied by the German merchants of the

Hanseatic League. They stand today, just as they stood five hundred years ago, their continuous roofline forming a saw-toothed edge against the sky, looking down, as always, on the quay (the Bryggen) and on the fish markets and the clustered masts of the fishing boats.

Immediately after breakfast we strolled down to the fish market. The waters of the slip were jammed with boats gleaming with fresh paint or with hulls of natural wood brightly varnished. In a great open space on the cobbled quay stone tables were set out, each fitted with a tank in which live fish nosed and pushed. This was the famous fish market. The vendors were mostly women as were the buyers. The former, ample of hip and bosom, stood poised for business, holding wicked knives with bloody blades. They looked as if they had just come from the French Revolution. The cobbles near the tables were darkened with bloodstained pools of salt water. It was a scene of picturesque violence.

An old woman holding a paper shopping bag puttered from table to table, peering into each tank and making an occasional remark to one of the fishwomen. Then she spotted her victim and pointed to it. A hand plunged into the water and seized the unhappy fish by the gills. With a single stroke its belly was slit and its innards deposited in a pail. Then, with equal deftness, the writhing carcass was rolled in an old newspaper and dropped into the housewife's bag where it gradually quieted down.

Sara and Lucy admitted that it was all very colorful, but seemed to think it was rather soon after breakfast for this sort of thing. We moved across the Bryggen to the row of Hanseatic warehouses.

Here are the quarters in which the German merchants of the fifteenth century made fortunes in ships' supplies and general trade goods, utilizing the labor of apprentices who, from all accounts, did not do so well.

They lived on the premises, these unfortunate lads, in quarters so cramped, so dark and so unsanitary that to one brought up in a unionized world, it seemed incredible that man could ever have obtained such domination over his fellow beings.

Here in these heavy-timbered, low-ceiled, dark old buildings, men lived out the circle of their narrow lives. Within these walls they worked and ate and slept and died. That phrase usually includes the word "loved," but Hanseatic apprentices were not permitted love lest through some amourette a bit of the profit should escape to a Norwegian wife.

Being practical people, their German masters allowed no woman to enter the premises. Even the old crones who made the beds of the apprentices could go no further than an outer hall where they had access to the built-in bunks through sliding panels too narrow (presumably) for apprentices or maids to wriggle through.

It struck us as curious that these boys, who were denied every possession, every ordinary comfort and who were little more than slaves, were never subjected to the final indignity of making their own beds, whereas today thousands of young bachelors, who at twenty-five have more possessions than most of the princes of old Baghdad, make their beds as a matter of course.

Although the roofs of the Hanseatic buildings present an unbroken front to the street, there are narrow alleys dividing them— romantic alleys with carved wooden balconies rising tier upon tier through the shadows and with great sails hanging between them as they have hung for hundreds of years. Had we come upon two men in hose and doublet, skewering one another with rapiers, it would have been entirely in keeping with the scene.

At this point Lucy and Sara left us. They wanted to go window-shopping and could stand this sort of thing no longer.

We had cocktails that evening with a charming and hospitable Norwegian family, and here for the first time we came into direct contact with people who had lived through an Occupation and had refused to submit in spite of all the odds against them.

We were going to see many more such people in Scandinavia and to take off our hats in respectful and wondering admiration for the particular brand of courage required by a resistance movement.

The soldier, ordered to advance against an enemy position, is carried forward by the presence of his companions on either side and by his fear of public opinion should he fail in his part while they are there to witness his failure.

The man in the resistance movement, however, has no familiar figures moving beside him to give him strength. He is alone in the dark. The chances are that if he turns and runs, no one will be the wiser, for his retreat is spiritual rather than physical. His objectives are not defined by a ridge or a clump of trees. They are vague and nebulous with no definite beginning or foreseeable end.

He cannot even be sure whether common sense and good judgment require the sacrifice which confronts him, or whether the results of the action which he contemplates are of sufficient importance to warrant the risks. It may well be that he has already done his share. Perhaps he now owes it to his family to bow his head to the gale and let it pass over him. It might even be best for his country.

He is faced with action of doubtful importance and attended by dreadful danger. If he is caught his fate is worse than that of the soldier struck on the battlefield, for he must suffer his end ingloriously and alone. A terrible price to pay for something of unknown value.

In the face of all these considerations, he takes the action and braves the danger. That is the kind of courage which is founded on faith.

6

Stalheim

IT WAS POURING WHEN WE LEFT BERGEN FRIDAY MORNING for Stalheim and the Sognefjord. The rain drove against our windshield in angry gusts as if trying to atone for its weakness in giving us two perfect days.

We had sat up much too late the night before and as a result it was not long before we wandered off on the wrong road. In fairness let it be said that it was one of the few times we lost our way on the entire trip, for the Scandinavians mark their roads with intelligence and frequency.

As usual when one is lost, all houses disappeared immediately; all traffic ceased. Eventually, however, a bus came over the brow of the hill behind us. I got out of the car and stopped it. When the door opened I asked the driver if he spoke English. Instead of reviling my ancestors and shutting the door in my face, as I had been trained to expect bus drivers to do, he said, "Nay." He then turned questioningly to his passengers.

An old gentleman arose, alighted from the bus and stood before me in the rain. In perfect Oxford he said that he spoke a little English—very little. We bowed. My bow was in deference to one who handled the old mother tongue better than I did.

I told him that we were lost. He gave me detailed directions, completely ignoring the driving rain, then, wishing us a pleasant sojourn in Norway, he turned to re-enter the bus. As he stood on the step smiling down at me, it would not have been surprising had he placed two fingers together and given a pontifical blessing.

The driver shut the door carefully. Everyone inside nodded and waved. The bus lurched on its way.

Back on the main road again, we retraced our route of Monday over the mountains east of Bergen. These mountain roads of western Norway are narrow. Perhaps in their narrowness lies their safety, however, for with a potential car approaching around every blind corner there is little temptation to exceed the Norwegian speed limits which go up to sixty kilometers where the road is open and the view unobstructed (neither of which conditions is ever met).

In most places there is just room for two cars to pass. On meeting, both usually stop, look over the ground, and then the one in the best position goes forward. In view of the fact that many of these encounters take place on roads which have been blasted out of the side of a cliff, this would seem to be a harassing experience for the outside driver—and it would have been if Norway had not done such a splendid job protecting its road edges.

The bad places are enclosed by miles and miles of low concrete walls about two and a half feet high, the inner side sloping out so that hubs will not strike when wheels come too close.

We had only one driving rule. When the person at the wheel became sleepy he did not try to be brave about it, but called for immediate relief. It seems incredible that one could think of sleep while driving through such scenery and on roads which could not hold to a straight line for more than a hundred yards in a mile. For some reason, however, the combination appeared to affect us like a sedative.

The first to give up the wheel was the lucky one. Even the second and third had reserves behind them. But when the fourth man took over and found himself watching the rolling heads of his traveling companions it gave him a lonely, "whence-all-but-he-had-fled" feeling. Who, he might well ask, was going to relieve him?

49

During the early days of the trip we still retained some vestige of self-consciousness. When overcome with sleep we turned our back to our seat companion, as far as that can be done in an automobile without dislocating the pelvis, and tried to hide our sagging jaws in the crooks of our arms.

That sort of idle vanity wore off quickly, however. Now, when the shut-eye relief took over, we let the head fall back and the jaw drop open for all the world to see.

There was something about the beating of the rain on the steel roof of the car that seemed to have a particularly soporific effect. We ran out of drivers as we approached Kvandall and stopped to revive ourselves with food.

The rain stopped also. Below us an arm of the fjord had narrowed down to a half mile. On the opposite shore the mountains rose almost straight from the water. Long, narrow pockets of snow lay across their crests like airfield markers.

Our road skirted the base of a mountain, purple-green with Norwegian pine. Kvandall was about half a mile down the grade, huddled at the water's edge. Some sort of a mill gave out a drowsy humming—no kind of a sound for us at that particular moment. Up the road someone was hammering. An occasional cyclist passed, turning to stare curiously at the car. Two little, tow-haired girls on one bicycle coasted down the slope, their legs stretched out stiffly. A man in a brightly mottled Norwegian sweater pumped up the hill without apparent effort, a child strapped into the little seat on the handle bars.

A motorcycle chugged past, ridden by a man with a girl clinging behind him. They were dressed in rubber suits which covered them from head to foot, and wore tight-fitting rubber helmets. Over their faces were plastic masks. They looked like visitors from Mars, but no good Norwegian will ride around the block on a motorcycle unless dressed cap-a-pie in rubber or leather and protected either by enormous goggles or a face mask. Only once did we see a man riding a motorcycle in a pair of ordinary pants and a shirt. By that time we were so acclimated to the Norwegian way of life that he looked indecent.

Ahead of us range after range of snow-capped mountains beckoned from the north. Eventually the waters of the fjord ended in the regulation pint-size village. Proceeding up the valley we found ourselves hemmed in by a gigantic headwall. It was hard to believe that we had not gone wrong for the second time that day. This must be a blind road ending at the wall, but the map showed differently.

We had not yet become accustomed to Norwegian road builders. Give one of them a good headwall and he will throw a road at it with the gusto of an American cowboy swinging a lariat at a calf. Just as our road threatened to terminate in some bushes under the cliffs, it found a miraculous toe hold on the granite face and started up like a goat.

Back and forth it crawled, each turn revealing new twists above and a long series of discarded twists below. At the top we passed under a railroad bridge. How the engineers had ever hoisted a railroad up to this place was hard to figure. We couldn't even guess *why*.

We were in the uplands again. Travel in Norway is like an ant's progress in an abandoned quarry. One climbs vertically to the mountain plateaus and then straight down again to water level. It is the kind of country that makes map distances deceptive.

A closed wooden gate barred the road. On the other side an infant viking in size-two rubber boots was racing madly to open it.

He was so small that he had to climb up on the gate rail to unlatch it. As we passed through he held out his hand. We stopped

51

and placed a few øre in it. He said *"Takk"* and shut the gate carefully behind us.

Very cute! Very picturesque! Then, in a quarter of a mile, we came to another gate, this one tended by two Norslings. We deposited øre with each and proceeded apprehensively. Our worst fears were realized. After half a mile we came to another. We were beginning to run out of øre. One more gate and we would be down to paper money. We had visions of motoring through the rest of Norway with our fountain pens out and our book of traveler's checks open on our laps.

Then we burst into the clear and the red clapboards of the Stalheim Turisthotel greeted us. This was not the last time that we were to run into the mystery of the multiple gates, but it was one that we never solved.

Stalheim stands on the edge of a tableland just at the point where the scenery shifts from mountaintop to water level in a single movement. It is a breathtaking place where one can sit on a bench in front of the hotel and look several thousand feet straight down into the canyon-like valley below.

Back and forth across the face of the headwall the road wriggles its way to the valley floor. There it joins the inevitable foaming stream, which takes a more direct route over the rim, and both go scampering down the canyon to the fjord, skirting the edges of a two-acre farm whose rows of hay driers look like pencil marks in the distance.

The porter came out to meet us and bowed his head reverently before our fourteen pieces of baggage. Inside the door he pushed a button. What must be the most beautiful chambermaid in the world (not in TV or musical comedy) appeared from somewhere and offered to show us to our rooms. She was dressed in black, with a little, frilled white apron and a cap to match, set on a head of golden Norwegian hair.

Stalheim is indeed a breathtaking place.

To reach our next stop we must drop into the narrow valley and follow it down to the village of Gudvangen at the head of the fjord. There, according to schedule, we were to take an early ferry for a long water trip to Balestrand.

It all seemed so easy until the porter told us that, on the following morning, the eight-thirty ferry was jammed to capacity. The next one did not leave until two-thirty in the afternoon and would not get us to Balestrand before midnight.

Now it really did not make any great difference whether we arrived at Balestrand at noon or midnight. True, it has the reputation of being one of the most beautiful spots in Norway, but certainly no place could be more beautiful than the one where we happened to be at the moment.

None of these philosophical thoughts occurred to us, however. Had we been in the middle of the Denakil Desert without water, we could not have been more eager to pull out on that first boat. We pleaded. We pounded the desk. We created fantastic reasons why we must get to Balestrand by noon come hell or high water. We indicated that bribery might be in the offing.

The porter was magnificent. He promised to investigate every impractical suggestion that we made. He did not even draw himself up proudly at the mention of special favor. He gave us his complete attention—and then did nothing further about it. Probably the unfortunate man had been obliged to watch this act twice a day for years.

The only good result of it all was that it made us ferry-conscious. We had learned finally, that space on a Norwegian ferry can be difficult to obtain. We made an immediate survey of all future ferries and then and there entered our telegraphic bids for reservations.

Ferry frustration had put us in a rather disgruntled mood when we gathered for dinner that night. Even the preliminary goblet of cold sherry brought us small comfort. Every available seat in the big living room was taken, and it is no great fun drinking chilled sherry standing up. It is not too much fun drinking chilled sherry sitting down.

We have said before that Norwegian food is excellent. It is. But Norway is obviously not a cattle country. The cattle have probably fallen off the ranges long since and broken their necks. Because of this, Norwegians do not seem to understand the preparation of meat as well as the cooks of New York, Buenos Aires, or Paris. In fact, Norwegian country cooks have a genius for making any piece of meat look like just that and nothing else.

I dabbed at the platter which the waitress (needless to say attractive) held before me. It contained small slices of brown, twisted flesh with an occasional odd-shaped bit of bone attached.

"What is this?" I asked, as irritably as one can sound when addressing a good-looking Norwegian girl. It might have been jerked camel's hump for all I could tell.

She seemed surprised at my question. Apparently no one had dreamed up such a crazy quiz before, but seeing that I was an American she gave the matter a moment's thought.

"It is, I believe, beef out of lamb."

I nodded understandingly. She was unquestionably attractive. Had she said beef out of shoe, I would have understood equally well.

That night a soft, cool breeze blew the turkey-red curtains into the bedroom and carried down the tinkle of cowbells and the distant roar of falling water from the slopes above.

When we came down to breakfast the next morning, rain was seeping through a heavy fog. The cowbells still tinkled. The falling water thundered more loudly than ever, but we could no longer see the sources. In some ways it was a relief. After the staggering, Valkyrian scenery of the past week it was restful to have nature draw the curtain momentarily and give us an intermission.

To make up for the lack of external interest, the Stalheim Turisthotel had concentrated on breakfast. It was laid out on a great table that must have been thirty feet long and ten feet wide and included, to our delight, shad roe and scrambled eggs and a meat that was almost unquestionably ham.

We could never understand how Norwegian hotels persuaded people to stay up all night preparing these enormous morning banquets. At home, Lucy calls our colored maid ten minutes after we get up and, by some culinary legerdemain, the latter manages to have orange juice, a cup of coffee and an egg ready for us when we hit the table a half-hour later. To prepare a Norwegian breakfast must take hours of loving labor and dozens of willing hands. In the kitchen, at any rate, the Scandinavian temperament must differ considerably from the American.

After breakfast we bought dozens of postcards and spent a good part of the morning writing furiously to people whom we wouldn't have crossed the street to speak to in the United States.

We were writing in a corner of the lobby. Every few minutes a diminutive English automobile or a great bus would pull up before the front door. The little cars looked just large enough to take one person if he curled up like a body prepared for a mound burial, but they usually disgorged from three to four full-sized adults, a poodle or two and an incredible amount of luggage.

Bus passengers did not carry so much baggage, but they made up for it in numbers. Each group entered the lobby giving out that high-pitched, defiant chatter to which shy people are apt to resort when entering strange places.

Around us sounded the multilingual babble of a foreign hotel. Each new inroad made a beeline to the porter's desk. At such moments he towered above the rabble, seeming almost superhuman. In the lulls between arrivals he was even able to take on a certain amount of social service work. An old lady came up to the desk.

"Have you seen my friend?" she asked.

He removed a stamp politely from the surface of his tongue before replying and handed out a room key from the rack behind him without turning to look.

"No, Madam, I haven't."

"I've been lying down," she said, "and my friend disappeared."

He placed another stamp on his tongue and bowed to the legion of forgotten friends who have disappeared in like circumstances. On the upswing of the bow he produced a package from under the counter and without a wasted motion took up the telephone receiver. It was a one-man ballet.

7

Balestrand

THE CLOUDS HAD MOVED ON TO RAIN IN OTHER PLACES, leaving only rear-guard wisps which stole along the steep sides of the mountains, probing cautiously into each ravine and gully.

A young man came staggering down the broad stairs, carrying all of our suitcases in one load. What means he used to attach them to his body we could not discover. He placed them on the ground behind the Plymouth, bowed, and disappeared.

We packed the car. "Where," we asked the porter who, in the intervals between licking stamps and passing out keys, had made out our bill, "is the young man who carried down our bags?"

"The young man who carried down your bags has gone to rest," he explained. There was a note of accusation in his voice as he turned to deliver a telegram to a moonfaced guest in a beret.

We dropped down the face of the narrow headwall on a corkscrew road which resembled a series of short toboggan runs—each ending in space.

It is only a short trip down the canyon to the fjord and the village of Gudvangen, where we were to take the ferry. This particular fjord was one of the innumerable arms which are common to Norwegian fjords. They all have special names. To us, however, it was our first look at the mighty Sognefjord which runs inland from the sea for 112 miles, flanked along the way by an honor guard of purple mountains.

Our ferry was waiting at the dock. So were about fifty automobiles, in spite of the fact that we had arrived a half-hour early.

Here was no ordinary ferry onto which one could drive from either end. In fact it did not look like a ferry at all, having all the lines of a trim little steam-yacht. Two-thirds of its eighty-odd feet were taken up with a neat mahogany cabin. Aft, were two decks. The lower one was already jammed with passengers, bicycles and hand baggage. To our amazement they were stowing automobiles on the upper.

A section of the railing had been temporarily removed and a long, steep gangway had been block-and-pulleyed up to it. At no point was the deck more than fifteen feet wide, so the little Austins and Morrises and Hillmans were placed in the bow where the beam was narrowest and the longer cars next to the cabin.

As each car was driven up the Noah's Ark ramp by its anxious-faced owner and came to an abrupt stop before plunging through the opposite rail into the fjord, its rear bumper was seized by three gigantic men who proceeded to rock the body up and down on its springs. When it had gathered sufficient impetus they caught it on the upstroke and literally heaved the wheels off the ground and threw the car laterally towards whichever side they wished.

Each twisting heave was good for a foot of side movement. Then they tackled the front bumper with equal gusto. Weight meant nothing to these lads. They shifted one car with all the passengers in it.

After a time it became easier to move the boat than to bounce cars, even taking into consideration the extraordinary indifference to hernia of Norwegian workmen. The lines were cast off and the ship moved forward ten feet to a point where another section of the rail had been removed.

It began to rain. No one paid any attention. No one in west Norway pays attention to rain at any time.

The slow process of loading went on. The passengers did not seem to mind the lack of progress in the least, but maintained the kind of animated chatter which characterizes the start of a boy scout jamboree.

We watched with double anxiety. In the first place it seemed obvious that not more than half of the waiting cars were going to get on the boat. In the second place we were not sure that we wanted to, for it was evident to us that they were putting all the weight in this slim-hipped carrier at least twelve feet above the water line, and it didn't take an engineer to foresee that when they untied the thing it would roll quietly over and point its streamlined smokestack at the bottom of the fjord.

The afterdeck was filled without an inch to spare. They moved the whole craft back and began to work on the forward deck. This was not a two-story affair, but it was built very high to give hold-room so that to anyone who was center-of-gravity conscious as we had become, it amounted to the same thing.

At this point Sara's passion for dumb creatures almost brought disaster. George, in a burst of generosity, had unearthed from one of his many duffel bags a confection called Buttercrisp. Simultaneously, Sara had discovered a goat. It was not much of a goat even when dry. Soaked with rain it was a highly repulsive specimen. Sara is the kind of a girl, however, who is not completely happy unless she is stuffing food into some animal. She naturally, therefore, took George's Buttercrisp and began putting it into the goat.

The miserable creature had obviously sprung from humble circumstances and was mad for this new taste sensation. To make things more convenient for Sara, he climbed into the rear seat beside her. Anyone but Sara would have noticed immediately that a wet goat is undesirable. She didn't.

At that moment the signal came from the boat for our car to come aboard. For the first time that afternoon they seemed to be in a hurry. Although the Plymouth Suburban is a remarkable car in every other respect, it is faultily engineered for unloading goats. It looked for a minute as if we were going to have to take Sara's conquest with us. George must have crawled into the back seat, however, and given him a particularly vicious bit of needling, for he suddenly emerged like a hairy cannon ball and disappeared in a panic around the corner of the ferry house.

On the deck we were packed in side by side with just enough room to open one door slightly and squeeze through, but there was no great temptation to do this for the rain was now coming down with an earnestness that only Norwegian rain can show.

They cast off the bow and stern lines. The top of the smokestack began to describe a slow arc away from the wharf. It was just as we had anticipated. We closed our eyes and waited for the moment when our car would be hurled into the icy waters of the fjord. But, somehow or other, we must have righted ourselves for when we opened them we had moved away from the dock, and the three giant workmen were engaged in the nice work of trimming ship by moving each car an inch or two backward or forward. It looked as if we might make it if there was no wind and everyone stood quite still.

We were running down the middle of a narrow fjord. On either side two-thousand-foot mountains towered above us, their flanks seamed with the thin white lines of cataracts. Here and there were tiny, shelflike bits of land, each supporting a mountain farm whose only access to the outside world was by water.

Then, as we moved further down the fjord, the mountains became too steep to support life of any sort and rose in sheer cliffs from the deep bottle-green water. A flock of terns followed us, mewing and doing exhibition-diving.

We looked at it all through the streaming windows of the car, settled ourselves as comfortably as possible and fell asleep. Viewed in retrospect it did not make too much sense. On the previous night, in a good bed and with the cards stacked in our favor, we had rolled and tossed sleeplessly. Now, passing through the most exciting scenery in the world, in the cramped and cluttered back seat of a suburban wagon, with our necks twisted dangerously out of shape, we slept like babies.

We left the ferry at Kaupanger, but the amphibious nature of our journey did not end there. Eleven miles later, at Sogndal, we took another ferry across a narrow arm of the fjord. This was a new type of transportation—a little scow affair which propelled itself mysteriously back and forth on two ropes.

At Leikanger we had supper at a small country hotel—great bowls of salad, meat which as usual was full of mystery but none the less palatable, a dozen kinds of rolls and bread, goat and cow cheese, sausages, cauliflower, carrots, various kinds of fish in tins, the inevitable fish pudding, tea and other odds-and-ends. When we came to pay, the bill was seventy cents each.

After this light refreshment we went on to Grinde where we waited for the little night steamer that was to take us on the last leg of our journey to Balestrand, a journey which from Stalheim could not have been over thirty miles by air.

It was another typically neat boat in spite of the fact that its cabin smelled overwhelmingly of fish. The smell of fish in Norway, however, has nothing to do with bad housekeeping. Fish is merely indigenous to the country as the hamburger is to the United States and spaghetti to Italy. In the bow, lounging among the anchor machinery and acting as a kind of spiritual air-wick, three beautiful blonde young women chatted with three beautiful blond young men.

It was eleven-thirty in the evening and almost dark. There was a strange sublight, however, which made everything stand out with the sharpness of a woodcut. The white outline of the Kvikne Hotel at Balestrand became visible, backed by snow-covered mountains and flanked by the silver arm of the fjord which turned to the right and disappeared behind a black promontory.

The Norwegians have an easygoing custom of bestowing several names on one place. Perhaps spots as beautiful as some of those on the west coast deserve this honor, but it is confusing to tourists with one-name minds. For example, Balholm and Balestrand are apparently one and the same. They both appear on the road map, separated by the tiny village of Ese. To make it harder the name of the hotel is Kvikne. The transom over the main entrance bears the painted legend "Balholm Hotel." In the United States most of the travel agents refer to the village of Kvikne—if they refer to it at all.

The same thing had been true of Ullensvang (which is a hotel) and Lofthus (which appears to be the village where the hotel is located). Both names are shown on the map, one above the other. Our original itinerary called for a two-night stop in Lofthus. We were later shifted to Ullensvang by the travel bureau and told that there was a better hotel there. We fought this bitterly at the time, as Lofthus had been particularly recommended to us.

The postman always rings twice in Norway.

We walked south along the shore of the Sognefjord on a narrow, orchard-bordered road. It was Sunday morning and the inhabitants of the village were returning from church in their holiday clothes. In the United States the road would have been crowded with automobiles, but in Norway one rides a bicycle or walks.

We passed the Episcopal church, built by the English colony in exuberant imitation of a Norwegian stave church, complete with tongue-sticking dragons—only, of course, these were English dragons. We stopped at the studio of the late Hans Andrea Dahl, who lived and painted for so many years in this locality and filled his charming old house on the shores of the fjord with his work.

And finally we sat on the rocks between the shore and the road, looking out over the broad waters of the fjord, shimmering in the noonday sun and ringed in the distance by misty mountains.

The steamer from Bergen passed and, as its wake eventually reached us, the seaweed rose and fell at our feet. It was the same kind of seaweed that rises and falls along the shores of the United States from Maine to Florida, and we suddenly realized what had been bothering us about Norwegian scenery. It was the mixture of seashore and mountains. At home we were more orderly about such matters. The mountains had their appointed place and the seashore had its. We were not accustomed to scrambling seaweed and snow-capped peaks and gulls and glaciers. It was confusing.

We were facing another of Norway's tremendous panoramas. If a man had any poetry, any philosophy in his soul, this was the place and time to call it forth. Sara and Lucy chose it as the setting for their daily discussion as to what they would wear for dinner. George chose it as a reminder of a miserable winter he had spent in a fishing village in north Italy. He described it in some detail to no one in particular. I chose it to doze with my back against a warm rock. The water lapped softly against the pebbles. A distant sea gull called. The world was a good place to be connected with.

After lunch we rented a Norwegian rowboat whose high bow and stern still retained the influence of its viking ancestors. The oars, indeed, might have come down through the centuries directly from the great seagoing ships. They were about ten feet long and together weighed almost as much as the boat.

A little fjord arm started beside the hotel and ended its career in about two miles at the foot of a wild-looking headwall. Over its rim melting glaciers poured their waters in two roaring white streams which met at the bottom, and tumbled over each other like eager puppies, scrambling to see which would first reach the salt waters of the fjord.

Sara and Lucy decided to row home. Each took an oar and we returned down the fjord in a circular, waltzing movement. It was late afternoon and the light was taking on that extraordinary amber quality which is so typical of Scandinavia. Around us the colors changed to delicate pastels while Sara and Lucy argued as to who it was that was pulling the boat in the wrong direction.

We drank our chilled sherry on the terrace and wished that we might have stayed a week in Balestrand (Balholm, Kvikne) instead of a day.

8

Loen

ON MONDAY MORNING WE PACKED THE CAR AND LET IT coast down a little flower-bordered alley to the dock. We were to take a steamer ferry to Ulvestad or Vetlefjord, it doesn't seem to make much difference to anyone which you call it—they are both on the map and they must be the same place, for there isn't room for two.

We were told that there would soon be a through road from Balestrand to Ulvestad, permitting motorists to omit this water leg. Perhaps it has already been completed. On a beautiful, sunny day such as this, however, it may not be too advantageous. There was a special crispness in the early morning air as we rounded the promontory, which had stood out so black and forbidding in the ghostly light of midnight two days before, and entered the tiny Vetlefjord which ended in a narrow slot between two sheer mountainsides.

On our left was a battery of magnificent waterfalls. A week ago we would have gone quite mad over such a sight and immediately ripped all the cameras from their cases. Norway had overdone this matter of waterfalls, however, and now it had to pay the penalty of our indifference.

We were much more interested in two big buses which were waiting at the landing, for at the same time that experience was making us waterfall-callous it was also making us road-cagey. It was evident in this case that in a few miles the road ahead must wind up the side of another great headwall where it would be impossible to pass a bus or anything else. We also knew that Norwegian buses and trucks are equipped with special low gears which enable them to crawl up these abnormal grades at an inchworm's pace. This means that if you get behind one of these slow-motion vehicles on a headwall climb, it is impossible to keep an ordinary car moving and there is nothing to do but stop and wait. While waiting you can amuse yourself speculating on what would happen if you could not get the motor started again.

So we raced away down the narrow main street of Ulvestad or Vetlefjord, ahead of the buses. As anticipated the road came quickly to a deep circular valley, looking like an enormous sugar bowl. There it turned to the left and fastened itself to the nearest headwall. We could trace its thin, white line rising, tier upon tier, among the gray rocks.

At the start of the climb, we passed, with some difficulty, a prewar sedan which was already in low gear and panting heavily. Each hairpin turn disclosed new beauties. Below us we could see the two buses coming upgrade behind the sedan, climbing slowly. Whether we could get out our cameras, take pictures and be off again before our pursuers caught up, developed into a kind of an outdoor guessing game in which the forfeits were high if we lost.

There would never be a dull moment as long as there was a roll of film left in the camera bag. People have asked if we did not sometimes get bored sitting in the car for so many hours. With four people whose tastes in photography were so positive and so different, the wonder is that we sat in the car long enough to complete the Scandinavian circuit.

Fortunately our disagreement as to what constituted a good shot was so fundamental that there was not enough common ground for argument. After the first few days it was an unspoken understanding that each should pursue his own impulses, however mad, without comment or innuendo from the others. It was a case of take and let take—and it worked, although it resulted in our coming home with almost seven hundred pictures.

Personally I belong to the album school of photography. To me pictures of places mean nothing unless they are associated with people. "That's Lucy and Sara leaning against the car. I don't know who the three children are. Yes, it was on one of the fjords. The fjord's on the other side of the car."

Lucy, left to her own devices, would have taken nothing but close-ups of flowers growing out of sod roofs or distant purple mountains, so far away that they would look like a smudge on the finished print.

Small animals of any kind always caused Sara to become a bit hysterical. We would be tooling along drowsily after lunch when she would see a yellow Norwegian pony and scream "Stop! For God's sake, stop!" Quite naturally whoever happened to be driving would slam on the brakes, causing the hand luggage, piled in the rear, to slide against the necks of the two people in the back seat. Sara would be out of the car before it skidded to a halt, a camera strap over each shoulder, shouting "It can't be over two weeks old!"

Whatever the immature animal was which had created this disturbance, it had usually disappeared over a hill by the time Sara came within range, so that she seldom succeeded in getting more than a blurred reproduction of its infantile hind end.

George's technique, on the other hand, was quite different. He had absorbed so much scenery during the course of his traveled life that he had become a connoisseur. His emphasis was on quality. A picture, he said, must have composition and balance or it was not worth the taking.

He usually discovered a subject which pleased him while we were on one of the rare stretches of straight road on which we could pick up a bit of momentum. "I think I'll take that," he would say, quietly. By the time the driver realized that George was not talking to himself, we would be a quarter of a mile down the road. This involved backing up and then removing the car to a place where it would not show in the picture. George would never tolerate the car in one of his compositions.

Once the car was out of his way he would pace thoughtfully back and forth in front of his subject, tilting his head this way and that and occasionally looking through the finder. Then he would climb several fences and attack the problem from different angles. Eventually he would signal to us to pick him up. "No good," he would grumble. "Terrible composition. Drive on."

There were times when we became quite provoked with him, particularly when it was late and we were getting hungry. On second thought, however, his method may have been the most intelligent of all. It gave him pleasure, it was by far the cheapest and he was saved all the subsequent agony of pasting prints in albums.

We were in the highlands again, passing through a wild, desolate region of mountains and rocks and black little lakes, surrounded by upland pastures.

Our faithful guide and mentor, Sydney Clark in his invaluable book *All the Best in Scandinavia* which shared the front seat with us throughout the trip, had told us that on this plateau it was possible to stop "at a mountain hut where travelers may enter a cowshed and buy, for about a dime, a vast bowl of yoghurt." Although we had no idea what yoghurt was, anything that came in a "vast bowl" and only cost a dime appealed to our sense of thrift. So we were on the lookout for likely-looking cowsheds.

We had been traveling for about half an hour without seeing so much as a hen coop, when we came to a collection of tumble-down sod huts. Nearby was a tiny, black-water lake surrounded by a pasture sprinkled with gigantic rocks. Two men stood in the midst of this chaos gloomily watching a dozen underfed cows.

We did not blame them for feeling depressed, but we all agreed that it was a photogenic scene. All, that is, except George, who said we would eventually discover that it had no central motif. The two men took great interest in us and kept pointing to the sod huts and mumbling in Norwegian.

Lucy said that they obviously wanted us to take a picture of them and that it was mean not to humor them, so, after we had finished photographing the cows and the rocks, we stood the men against the wall of one of the huts and let them have it from all angles. Instead of being grateful they looked more dour than ever. We decided that loneliness had soured them and went away.

It was several hours before we realized that this must been the place where we might have bought the vast bowl of yoghurt for a dime. I would not care to be the next traveler who gets out in that wild, rock-strewn upland and starts taking pictures.

The very magnificence of the Norwegian scene became a source of constant danger to us. We would be driving along a narrow road with a sheer drop on one side and a cliff on the other. Even though the outer edge of the road was protected by the usual low coping, it was no place for a driver to go sight-seeing. At just such moments, however, Sara or Lucy was sure to scream: "Look, look!" upon which everyone, including the man at the wheel, would crane his neck to take in some new wonder five hundred feet above or below.

We finally overcame this menace by entering into a solemn agreement under which anyone spotting a remarkable bit of scenery was to place his finger on his lips, touch his two companions, who were not driving, on the shoulder and point silently. In this way the man at the wheel was not let in on the matter at all, and we remained intact.

Among its many other attributes, Norway is the hand-wavingest country in the world. After a long day on the road, one's wrist is weary from returning the waves of little tots in rubber boots, peasant girls in rubber boots, farmers in rubber boots, and old folk in rubber boots. One would think that these people, living in such lonely places, would resent the swift flight of a motor car whirring gaily past and leaving them again to their solitude. Even if they did not resent it, one would suppose that they must tire of saluting each passing vehicle.

Their enthusiasm is boundless, however. At the sound of the motor little children ran to the side of the road, workers stopped hanging wisps of hay on drying wires, old folk came to the doorways. One and all waved their greeting and we returned it unflinchingly.

We lunched in the original Bosky Glen beside a beautiful lake. Great trees rose from a rich carpet of green moss. George tied a string to the shutter lever of his enormous camera and took a portrait of himself. It was one of the first pictures he had taken in days.

At the eastern end of the Nordfjord the Hotel Alexandria stands in an amphitheater of blue-gray mountains. The hotel is about all there is to Loen, but the rambling, white, Victorian structure, offering every comfort in the midst of all this lonely grandeur, seems quite sufficient unto itself.

It was raining the next morning. Low clouds truncated the surrounding mountains. We drove to Loen Lake and the Kjendal glacier. Up to this point we thought we had seen the tops in scenery, but Norway seems to be able to maintain a continuous crescendo. The narrow lake forces itself between the mountains, to be fed by the great glacier at the point where the latter lunges over the edge of the escarpment.

These are no ordinary mountains, but cliffs rising thousands of feet from the shores of the lake. The narrow road had a difficult time finding a foothold between rock and water, but in spite of this there were the inevitable Norwegian farms, diminutive affairs, a couple of acres and a few sod-roofed huts, their owners subsisting on God-knows-what. A Norwegian farmer is so constituted, apparently, that wherever he finds a bit of more or less level ground, there he will establish a farm even if he had to get to it by helicopter.

Near the inner end of the lake rises the Ravnefjell, a rocky cliff over sixty-five hundred feet in height. It is composed of what is locally known as "rotten rock" and every so often a great mass breaks loose and plops into the lake.

In the over-all, this is perhaps no more important than the breaking off of a clod of earth from the side of a water hole, but to the people who own the little farms around the lake, it is tragedy and death, for Loen Lake is almost four hundred feet deep and when these great rock masses fall into it, the resulting waves eliminate the farms and those who have struggled so valiantly to maintain them.

Such breaks occurred in the winter of 1905 and again in the fall of 1936, causing the deaths of 150 farmers and their families and throwing a small lake steamer five hundred feet up a wooded slope where it remains today—a monument to a tragic splash.

As we followed the twisting shoreline the shoulders of the cliffs ahead of us appeared to converge and actually overlap at their bases. It was like a stage-set for some Gargantuan opera. Half a mile from the head wall was a lonely restaurant. There, out of the rain, we could watch the green ice of the glacier spilling over one corner of the wall, to grind its way down the sloping shale in a great serpentine curve.

71

9

Geiranger

OUR BREAKFAST TABLE AT THE ALEXANDRIA STOOD BESIDE
a broad plate-glass window looking westward down the Nordfjord.
The rain had stopped. Far down the fjord the sun burst suddenly
through the clouds, setting ablaze the distant snow slopes. Beauty
on such a scale has some of the qualities of organ music echoing
through the vaulted dimness of a medieval cathedral.

Lucy and Sara sat side by side soaking it all in through dreamy,
half-seeing eyes. Ordinarily they were both inclined to flippancy
in the early morning, but Nature had apparently subdued them
for the moment. They were talking in low tones, eagerly, like
women inspired.

"What are you talking about?" asked George, who hates to be
left out of a conversation.

"Our hair," said Sara.

It is only eighty miles from Loen to Geiranger, but they are
eighty of the most memorable miles in the world.

It was raining, as usual, when we left the Alexandria. Our road
wound around the shoulder of a mountain and picked up the
mouth of the boisterous, salmon-filled Stryn which it followed
to Stryn Lake. This is an amazing little body of water, jammed
into the end of a narrow valley and almost surrounded by
precipitous mountains which crowd to its shores like a herd of
thirsty, prehistoric monsters. Perched on its inner edge, at the point
where the road begins to wind up the pass, is the tiny village of

Hjelle. It consists of a few houses and a charming little hotel whose balconies overhang the glacier-green water. No one has mentioned this place in the guidebooks. There are no photographs of it in the tourist offices. We decided then and there, however, that on our next trip to Norway, Hjelle would be on our list and that we would drink chilled sherry on one of those balconies.

The road started up the pass like the take-off of a fighter plane. Actually it wasn't so much a pass as a cleft between two mountains, so narrow that only a few yards separated one hairpin turn from the next. The ultimate top was hidden by the clouds. Hjelle became a speck below us and Stryn Lake turned into a puddle, barely seen through the slanting rain. We were suspended in mid-air in a slot between granite mountainsides, their ravines filled with snow.

At Oslo it had been decided to make one member of the party temporary treasurer and disbursing agent. We had elected George to this job "just for a day or two." He was, unfortunately for him, so good at it that we never let him off the hook until we returned to New York.

Up to this point George had told us little about our financial status. He now chose this particular spot to make an oral audit. It appeared that there were certain cash dividends due us on borrowings he had made from the pool. It was never clear, but as we ground around the blind turns, praying that no mountain bus might come bounding down the grade, he distributed kröner to each with elaborate explanations. Perhaps he felt that in a few moments kröner might be quite useless.

In the midst of the climb we came upon a small inn with the big name of Hosslidarveider. It clung to the edge of nothing at a widening of the twisting road and was strapped to the ground by thick cables which passed over its slate roof. It was literally a house tied to the side of a mountain.

The rain barred photography so we left Hosslidarveider quickly

73

behind and below, and continued our endless ascent through the mist until we finally emerged into an upland country where the snow still clung in soggy drifts six to eight feet deep. We were on the top of the range, in the region where the phrase "desolate loneliness" must have been coined.

Grotli, a hotel where one changes buses at a wilderness crossroad, seemed an intruder in this rocky chaos. We ate our picnic lunch in the car that day. Up here above the timber line there was no temptation to loll around even though the rain had stopped.

Eventually we reached the point where the tableland ended and the road started its long drop to the Storfjord and Geiranger. It was an enormous twister, so big that the engineers had apparently grown discouraged and left off most of the outside wall. Danger seemed to bring out the best (or was it the worst?) in George who happened to be at the wheel. He began to crane his neck out the window in order to get a better look at points of interest. He hooked the fingers of his left hand into the car gutter and drove with one hand. At one point he even removed that from the wheel to light a cigarette. He told us gay stories of a winter spent in Czechoslovakia. For once, Sara and Lucy did not dare to interrupt.

Geiranger is the Mecca for Norwegian publicity photographers, for here Norway reaches a scenic climax with all the kettledrums in action. At Geiranger the mountains are bigger. They rise straighter from the water. The streams thunder louder. It is a good place to be, rain or shine.

On the slope, just above the little village, the Union Hotel stands beside a particularly articulate bit of white water and looks out over the fjord as it has done for the greater part of a century.

After dinner that night the rain ceased for a moment and we walked up the headwall road. It does not take much effort to unearth a view in this country. At the end of twenty minutes

Geiranger had resumed its role of a toy village and the water of the fjord had turned into a silver mirror.

The world at water level had become unreal. The torn wilderness above us was hidden by rain clouds. We were in a region which did not belong to the top nor to the bottom—a neither-nor kind of a place where all values were measured vertically rather than horizontally.

It would have been an excellent locale for eagles and giant condors who wanted to get away from things and do some brooding— but man, in his unceasing struggle to make things harder for himself, has staked his claim first. All around the semicircle of mountains were diminutive farms crouching on shelves of earth like climbers who have reached a point where they do not dare to go either up or down. This was where Mark Twain became the travel writers' friend by remarking that the children in these regions had to be tied to the farms to keep them from falling off.

Later that evening the genial proprietor of the Union Hotel told us that some of these farms had been in the same family for hundreds of years. In many cases the farm buildings had been carried away by avalanches, not once but several times. Always, he said, the buildings had been replaced, but during the last few generations the tenants had fallen into the habit of moving out during the avalanche season. The tone of his voice indicated that he deplored this modern trend to softness.

Nothing changes rapidly in Norway. The Union Hotel, like so many others of its kind, has been owned and managed by one family for so long that everyone is getting rather vague about when it all started. Queen Victoria and the Prince Consort came there once with their large retinue. The proprietor showed us their signatures with pride. It had been an old hotel then.

He told us that the place "closed itself" in September with the falling of the first snow. Then the soft white flakes draw a misty curtain over the headwall which cuts off the little village from the world except by way of the fjord.

He pointed to a promontory down the fjord which was just visible in the dim light. "The village *is* the world during those months," he said, "and, when the conversation wanders too far afield and tends to become heated on subjects we can't hope to know much about, the villagers have a saying, 'Don't go past the point.' It saves many arguments."

When the last tourist has left and the village knows that its privacy is secure, it casts off all pretenses, loosens its necktie, and reverts to the ancient customs which have prevailed in the district for a thousand years.

Not the least of them is the selection of a Beer King. Early in the fall, each household sets hopefully about the brewing of beer according to family formulae which have been handed down through the generations. When all is in readiness, the villagers go on a sampling tour from house to house and, on the basis of their findings, elect a King.

It appeared to us a dubious distinction, as we were given the impression that it was the King's prerogative to furnish all the good folk of Geiranger with free beer for the balance of the winter. Quite obviously, therefore, each aspirant to the throne must brew enough beer for the entire village—just in case. It was not an economical system, but one which at least ensured against a shortage.

And then in the spring the avalanches roar from the mountains above the village, the wet ones slow and noisy, the dry ones fast and silent. The owners of the little farms which are in line of fire find it a good time to visit their relatives. People begin to paint and tidy up and the sound of hammers echoes through the fjord in anticipation of the day when the headwall road will again be open and tourists will begin to come twisting down to leave their offerings in the ancient tills of Geiranger.

We had prayed for good weather, but there was something the matter with our technique, for the next morning it was still raining. As a solace the Union Hotel put on a breakfast of Oriental profusion and diversity. We had learned discretion, however. The days when we took a dab of everything were behind us. Now we were satisfied with a dish of rhubarb, some chilled scrambled eggs and sliced ham, breaded roe, crackers and marmalade, washed down by three cups of coffee.

About eleven the rain stopped. The proprietor had told us of a new road that was being built to the village of Yterdal, which he thought we might find on the sensational side as far as it had gone. We decided to explore it. Fortunately for our nerves, it had not gone far.

It climbed across the face of a mountain which rose almost vertically from the fjord, struggling upwards in a series of hairpin curves. This was truly a narrow road being only wide enough for one car with occasional turn-off places for passing. As the road was under construction, there were few, if any, guard rocks on the outer edge. Geiranger and the fjord sank further and further down (straight down) and the temptation to look over the edge became less and less.

Even here, clinging to the mountainside were farms whose log and sod-roofed buildings might have been put together by the vikings. Cables, operated by hand winches, connected them with the water below and all merchandise, whether imported or exported, must pass over this route.

At last we came to the end of the road construction. It was not a place that one would have chosen for turning. At the outer edge the mountain fell off straight to the fjord several thousand feet below. Fortunately the roadmakers had dug into the embankment on the inside so that at this particular point, we had a width of about fifteen feet to fool around in.

77

I backed the car as far as I could against the embankment. The next move involved driving head-on for the open edge. This was too much for any of us. We walked up the road over the broken stones until we found some light logs. These we placed along the edge. A child could have kicked them over, but they were psychological rather than physical barriers. We turned the car around and started down to more stable ground.

On the way, during one of our frequent halts for picture-taking, we met a Dane. He had long teeth and a long, pointed nose and might have posed for Brother Wolf in a book of children's stories. He carried a great armful of flowers. Stopping abruptly before Lucy and Sara, he presented each of them with a double handful of wild lilies. Then he made a little speech in English saying that this gift came from his heart as a mark of gratitude for what President Truman had done for world peace. He terminated this address with a deep bow and strode away down the road. Lucy and Sara were almost in tears. They took the tribute quite personally, and were not used to this kind of knight-errantry on country roads.

On the previous day, just before we had descended from the escarpment to Geiranger, we had passed what is known as The Dalsnibba. This is literally a mountain on top of a mountain. It sits on the edge of the great plateau which dominates Geiranger and pushes the earth's surface twenty-four hundred additional feet into the air. It is by no means the highest point in Norway, but it certainly ranks as one of the most sensational, looking out over a sea of mountain peaks and glaciers.

The Dalsnibba is reached by a private road. Late in the afternoon the rain stopped and we decided to retrace our steps up the headwall and drive to the summit.

Shortly after we had left the Geiranger-Grotli road and paid our toll to a charming Norwegian girl, whose social life in this outlandishly remote spot must have been somewhat restricted, the clouds closed in on us again. The road wound up and up. We had the feeling that we were leaving the earth below us on a path which would never end its ascent. Elijah in his chariot must have felt somewhat the same way.

Then at last, we came suddenly to the top. It consisted of a parking area and an observation platform, the latter built out over space. We tiptoed gingerly onto the platform, gripping the railing. At that moment the clouds rolled away, disclosing for an instant yawning nothingness below and in the distance peak after jagged peak. Then the clouds closed in again. We had seen enough and returned to the car and the security of the Union Hotel.

10

Trondheim

WE WERE STARTING THE LAST LEG OF OUR NORWEGIAN journey—from Geiranger to Trondheim. A bit of sunshine on this final day in the big fjord country would have been a friendly gesture, but the weather was like a child which has worked itself into a tantrum and does not know how to stop. The rain was driving viciously against the windows of the dining room as we ate our breakfast at seven-thirty and the general tone of things was on the moody side.

Our day was scheduled to start with a long ferry trip. Following the custom of the house, the proprietor came down to the dock to wish us bon voyage. There was no question about its being a wet one, but our friend's national disregard for the weather was so complete that he did not even bother to wear a raincoat.

This was an orthodox little ferry which carried its cars where ferries should and gave no indication that it had once been a proud mine sweeper. That did not mean that it had fallen into sloppy ways, however, for like all Norwegian ferries it looked as if it had been painted the night before.

Our host spoke to the captain and we were invited to take refuge from the rain in the pilot house—the equivalent, in these waters, of being asked to sit at the captain's table.

We crowded into the tiny structure with a large group of other damp and honored guests, in addition to the helmsman and a youth with a disarming grin and a portable mike, whose task it was to describe the scenery over a loud-speaker system and to act as a marine disk jockey.

He was an earnest young man who took his job seriously. Having commented on a waterfall, first in English, then in Norwegian, he would burrow frantically through the congestion to the captain's cabin muttering: "Oh, oh, I must make some music. Excuse it please."

We went waltzing away from the dock at Geiranger to the strains of the "Blue Danube" which reverberated from the mountainsides and went rolling down the fjord ahead of us. Then, after a bilingual description of the Seven Sisters Falls, he set the mike carefully on the window sill and in a few moments the first notes of "Ave Maria" blasted the startled sea gulls slightly off their courses.

It was crowded in the wheelhouse and a bit on the steamy side. Each time the helmsman moved the wheel, one of the spokes dug into the ribs of a passenger. No American captain would have been so foolhardy as to admit such a crowd even if there had been a typhoon outside. He would have known that eventually someone would pull the controls to the engine room, hang on the whistle cord, or otherwise disrupt the orderly progress of his vessel.

But Scandinavians seem to be more mature in these matters. The passengers listened attentively to the intermittent lectures, even including the part in English which most of them could not understand. During the musical period they chatted quietly. Occasionally they left the wheelhouse to go out and stand in the rain.

Quite evidently these people had either been born waterproof or else, like plants, they felt the need for being watered frequently. It was a cold, driving downpour which in any other country would have sent everyone under shelter. To our fellow passengers, however, it might have been a bright, sunny day. They stood about the decks in animated groups, holding lighted cigarettes under their cupped hands and punctuating their chatter with quiet laughter, oblivious of the water rolling down their necks.

High up on the side of a mountain, where breaking rock had created a bit of level ground, was a rain-soaked farm. No road connected it to the outside world, only a cable slanting steeply to the water's edge and a corkscrew path. It was the sole habitation in sight on either side of the fjord—a pinpoint of orange-red in a savage world of rocks and icy, gray-green water; the symbol, the bellwether, of all the thousands of lonely farms which have clung to these cliffsided mountains for so many centuries.

We docked briefly at a little town by the name of Stranda. It was the first industrial center that we had seen in Norway and probably one of the few places in the world which uses only electricity to move its machinery and heat its houses. According to our guide there was not a coal furnace in the place. As we pulled away from the dock the sun broke through the clouds momentarily. Stranda's houses and factories gleamed and sparkled against the brilliant green of the hills behind them. It was an impressive testimonial to electricity.

At Sylte, we said good-by to Norwegian ferries and started up the Valdal toward Åndalsnes. In this country where any old gorge can qualify as a valley, the Valdal comes under the classification of "broad and fertile." Here were the largest farms, the most extensive fields, the biggest barns we had seen since leaving the United States; Norway had somehow stepped out of its role and we were inclined to resent it.

At a roadside stand we bought a great basket of fresh strawberries and lunched in the car on crisp-crusted bread, cheese, fresh butter, marmalade, and berries, while the rain drummed on the metal roof. Then, as if wearied of its efforts to be civilized, the road plunged into a narrow pass and began to wind steeply upward. It was Norway again, and we relaxed.

Suddenly, and without any preliminary build-up, we came to what might have qualified as one of the outstanding panoramas of the trip if it had not been so rain-soaked. We were on the edge of a tremendous headwall. Far below lay the valley, a mile-wide strip of dark green fenced in on both sides by mountains. Beside us a small lake lapped the rocky rim of the headwall like a placid kitten and then, with suicidal suddenness, plunged into the valley.

A platform had been built out over the edge for those who enjoy looking down into emptiness. It disclosed the pretzel-like lines of our road which, after writhing in agony halfway down the wall, finally crossed the falls and crawled behind some rocks—presumably to die.

Unfortunately, we had not acquired the rainproof quality of Norwegians. Water running out of our hair into our eyes still offset dramatic effects and we sloshed back to the car. Norway had put on its last big show. The scenic *Götterdämmerung* was over. We sensed it and were depressed as we put the Plymouth in low gear and nosed over the rim.

The Grand Hotel Belleview at Åndalsnes is smaller than its name, but it compensates for its lack of size in many ways. For one thing it was the only new hotel we found in Norway. It was new for the simple reason that the unfortunate town was practically obliterated by bombing during World War II. As a result, most of its buildings had to be new, or else.

We took our evening walk of exploration, ducking intermittent showers. Near the railway station we kibitzed a Norwegian funeral in the face of violent protests from Lucy and Sara, who couldn't have been removed from the scene with anything short of a bulldozer.

The funeral services were being held in some sort of public building. The hearse was waiting in front and it was this vehicle that had first caught our attention. Basically, it was an open Sears Roebuck farm wagon which had been painted in intricate designs and surmounted by an ornamental wooden canopy, supported by four elaborately carved, wooden posts.

83

This open-air hearse was drawn by a single horse—an animal without apparent ambition, for it had quite shamelessly gone to sleep; and its driver, who leaned against the hearse, seemed on the point of following suit. Lucy and Sara said that it was a breach of international courtesy to stand there and stare. They had taken up positions in front of a hardware-store window where they could examine carpenters' tools without missing a detail.

The service was over. The pallbearers emerged, each carrying a raincoat over his free arm. With some difficulty the coffin was slid over the tailboard of the hearse. The driver awoke and in turn aroused the Norwegian pony by the simple device of starting down the road and pulling it after him.

The procession started. The mourners fell in behind the hearse, three and four abreast. Through the rain they walked slowly, around the corner, up a hill, finally disappearing down a wooded side road.

On the next morning we left for Dombås following the narrow Romsdal as it twisted through the mountains. On our right the Rauma River roared its unruly way down to the fjord.

Lucy and Sara had heard somewhere that between Åndalsnes and Dombås lay Norway's Great Divide. I don't know why this bit of geographical data interested them so much, but it had apparently left a deep impression. We would reach a point, they explained, where the river would suddenly start to run the other way and each time they caught sight of the Rauma they craned their necks to see if it had reversed its flow.

George and I received all this with that pained attitude which is the only male defense against imbecility and, as usual it eventually reduced Lucy and Sara to a proper state of inferiority.

Later we read in Harlan Major's excellent book *Norwegian Holiday* that at Lake Lesja, which lies halfway between Åndalsnes

and Dombås, the Rauma River flows from its western end toward
Åndalsnes and the Lågen starts from the east end and goes foaming
off in the opposite direction. We never told Lucy and Sara about
this, as they are the kind of women who harbor such inconsequential episodes and use them again and again to one's disad-
vantage.

Somehow or other a railroad had been built between Åndalsnes
and Dombås to connect the port city with the main line running
north from Oslo. It was not an ordinary railroad, winding placidly
up a mountain valley. There was not a placid tie in its whole
structure. Its tracks took the impossible grades in great loops and
double loops. At one point three rights-of-way were in sight at the
same time, one above the other. It was the kind of a railroad that
darts into mountains, makes a complete turnabout and darts out
again going in the opposite direction.

It flirted all the way to Dombås, disappearing into the side of a
hill far below us on the right and reappearing above us on the
opposite side of the road. It was the coyest railroad we had ever
had anything to do with. Had it waved a signal arm and yoo-hooed
we would not have been surprised.

We spent that night in Dombås and on the following morning
left for Trondheim. The road immediately climbed to the Dovre
plateau, an enormous expanse of nothingness dominated by the
Snøhetta whose icy cone was shrouded by the leftovers from last
night's rain.

Sydney Clark says about Trondheim that it is "for travelers, a
stone cathedral with a wooden city around it"—the last of the great
wooden cities of Norway, standing only three degrees below the
Arctic Circle.

But it is more than just a wooden city. It is the birthplace of a nation, the battleground on which were staged the final struggles between paganism and Christianity in the north countries, the starting point of Leif Eriksson's expedition which eventually wound up on the shores of North America, the burial place of kings, and the Mecca of pilgrims for a thousand years.

Its history is inextricably tied to that of the great cathedral which dominates it and which was started about the time that William the Conqueror was trying to make up his mind whether he dared have a go at England. Work on it is still being pushed forward vigorously and it would seem that, barring unforeseeable delays, another thousand years should see the job completed.

The original purpose of the cathedral was to house the remains of Olav Haraldsson, the doughty Christian king who might very well have ended by killing all his subjects in the process of converting them to the true faith, if he had not come out on the wrong side of a religious argument and ended by being killed himself.

Death could easily have meant historical oblivion for Olav Haraldsson as it has for many other worthy people if, for an unexplained reason, someone had not dug him up about a year after he was buried beside the river Nid—and found him in prime condition.

The Pope, quite naturally, canonized Olav and the cathedral was started, as a matter of course, shortly after.

It was late afternoon when we arrived in Trondheim. We wandered about in a shutter-happy mood, taking pictures of the cathedral, the hoary old buildings which surround it, the ancient warehouses lining the river and the even more ancient dwellings on its eastern shore.

We climbed the hill to the old fort, Kristiansten, and looked down over the city and the fjord as men have looked down on them for ten centuries. Time rolled back. We were the soldiers of Olav

Trygvasson guarding the sea approaches to the new settlement. We were the friends of Leif Eriksson watching his longboats head for the setting sun. We were——

The keeper of the old fort and his attractive wife approached us. He lifted his cap politely and pointed to a slab of concrete half-hidden by the thick grass. On the wall behind it was a bronze plaque. "Here," he said, undramatically, "is where the Germans shot Norwegians. They stood facing the wall, so. The soldiers stood here." Time rolled forward and the terror of a recent Occupation cast its shadow over the mossy walls of the enclosure.

The story of Trondheim and its famous cathedral has been well and fully told by others. We dined that night in the great, old-fashioned dining room of the Britannia, watching its fountains rising to the colored skylights. The food was excellent, the music good. Time inched forward another notch and wars were something one read about in books. In the world of reality all was peaceful and secure.

It was eleven o'clock when we left the table. Outside it was still twilight. I bought a newspaper at the concierge's desk and read it as George and I strolled about the town. We could not understand what it said, but it gave us both great pleasure to be reading Norwegian by daylight at midnight.

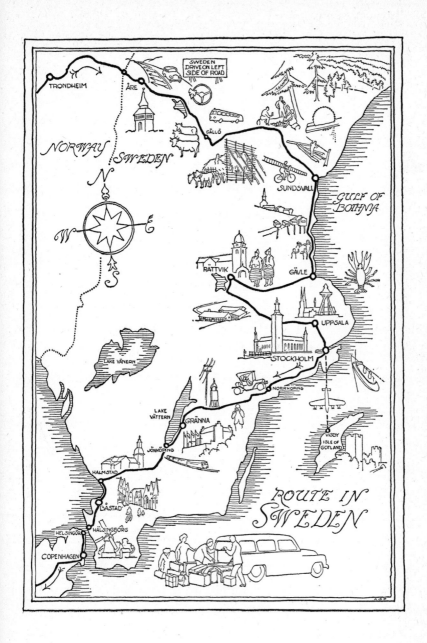

Sweden

11

Åre

ON TUESDAY MORNING WE HEADED NORTHWEST FROM Trondheim to the Norwegian-Swedish border and the skiing center at Åre, Sweden, approximately 130 miles away.

Norway has more costumes than a debutante and shares the latter's fondness for changing them constantly. On leaving Trondheim we came into open, rolling country which might have been transplanted from New England. On our left we had occasional glimpses of the blue water of Trondheimsfjord, but this was no rock-walled eagle's sanctuary, such as we had been accustomed to, but a trained and docile body of water on whose tranquil shores children sailed toy boats.

It was the type of scenery which aroused all the non-picture-taking instincts in George. "Look," he would exclaim excitedly, "there's a fine shot—that white church with the red barn just below. Jove, what a picture!"

"Want to stop?" the driver would ask, without slowing down.

"No, no," George would answer hastily, "but if there were cloud effects above that church, I'd take it in a minute. I wouldn't hesitate."

We passed the village of Hell without unnecessary comment and a few miles further north, at a hamlet carrying the equally improbable name of Stiklestad, we left the main road and turned east. We did so regretfully, for ahead lay the North Cape and Lapland and all that region of mystery which lies above the Arctic

Circle. But it was all hundreds of miles away and a very different trip.

We approached the Swedish border with some misgiving, knowing that here we must switch from the right-hand side of the road to the left. The formalities on the Norwegian side were few. Having filled out the usual questionnaire and exchanged the customary bows we were waved jovially on our way.

On the previous evening a friend in Trondheim had suggested that when we came to the border we should tie a handkerchief on the left-hand side of the steering wheel to remind ourselves that the rules of the road had changed. We thought this an excellent idea and used one of George's best to carry it out. Then we inched the car over to the left-hand side and started cautiously eastward.

The door of the customhouse flew open and a young man in uniform rushed out screaming. We jammed on the brakes and reached guiltily for our driver's license. The young man was much disturbed. Were we Swedish, he said, to drive so on the left? We must drive on the right until we came to twelve kilometers. Then, and then only, were we to left-switch.

There was some doubt in our minds as to what country we would be in while traveling those twelve kilometers. We also wondered if people coming in the opposite direction knew about this no man's land and, when a big bus came thundering around the corner, we drove the car off the road without a moment's hesitation.

At the eastern end of no man's land we came to the Swedish customs. A cross young man examined our papers minutely. He then had a long conversation with another morose youth. They went to the window several times and examined our car. Eventually, the first one pointed out to us in a tired voice that all automobiles must have *two* licenses, one in front and one in back. He indicated that in Scandinavia the youngest children were aware of these basic facts of life.

We pointed out that we were carrying a Norwegian license in front and back. He rebutted triumphantly that we carried our American license in back only. We explained that in New York State it was the law at that time to carry only one license plate. He smiled at us for advancing such silly ideas. Other American cars had two licenses. Who were we to be different?

At that moment, unfortunately, an Illinois Chrysler came to rest outside the customhouse. The cross young man pulled me to the window.

"There," he said, "you see? That proves. They have two plates. They know the law. You cannot enter Sweden with one license."

It is hard to tell what might have happened if a ruddy-faced young inspector had not entered the room at that moment. We took out our wallet and flashed our Blue Cross card at him. It seemed to impress him.

"Won't you talk to *him?*" we pleaded, sensing a kind heart. There followed an interminable conversation with much peering through the window. Finally, all three inspectors came to the counter like Dumas' Musketeers and waved toward the interior of Sweden.

"Go," they said. "Go. And God help you when the police they see you."

We drove into Sweden nervously, clinging to the left-hand side of the road. At each corner the back-seat drivers took up a rhythmic chant of "Left, left" and all conversation ceased as we concentrated on that one vital concept.

The handkerchief was undoubtedly helpful except for the fact that, when turning corners, it suddenly showed up on the right-hand side of the wheel. This was disconcerting.

Our Trondheim friend had also reassured us with the information that in the north country of Sweden we would meet many large trucks the drivers of which, he had said, traveled at great speed and in rounding corners almost invariably used the wrong side of the road (from the Swedish point of view). He warned us that when we met one of these Juggernauts, our instinct would be to get to the side of the road where in the United States we normally belonged. The Swedish driver would do the same for Sweden and the ultimate result would appear in one of the Stockholm papers.

Like most of the gratuitous information which we picked up about the trip, this was quite erroneous. We did not meet many trucks. Those we did were traveling fast, but they were not on the wrong side of the road. They were in the exact middle. So there could be no confusion.

There is a wealth of misinformation available for the asking (frequently without it) to the prospective motorist in Scandinavia. We had been told, for instance, that Swedish roads were built on the principle of washboards. Our informant had advised strongly against bringing our own car, assuring us that it would be shaken into bits and scattered along the roadside before we were halfway down the peninsula.

We had been told that the roads were badly surfaced and that we would drive in a constant cloud of white, suffocating dust.

As for the secondary roads, we had been warned to stay away from them at all cost. One had the feeling that, rather than take a secondary road, it would be preferable to strike off across the fields.

Apparently none of our advisers had done much traveling in Sweden since the days of Gustavus Adolphus. We found the roads, both main and secondary, excellent and dustless in all three countries.

The road wound through long stretches of pine and hemlock. For our money we might have been approaching Lake Placid in the Adirondacks. Around five o'clock we reached Åre, which was so small that we went through it without noticing and had to back up. We all agreed that it would be pleasant to live in a place where one could get into the country so quickly from the middle of town.

The Åregården Hotel is built primarily for the ski trade. Its plate-glass windows, set in walls of heavy logs, look out over the surrounding slopes and the white water of the ever-present mountain stream. It is a pleasant spot, winter or summer, where (let the traveler be warned) one can obtain the world's strongest Martini.

Our efforts to dig up a good cocktail in Scandinavia were as unflagging as they were usually unproductive. It was a problem which had not troubled us in Norway where so few places had liquor licenses. In Sweden and Denmark, however, licenses were more numerous, but knowledge of the bartender's art seemed to be largely confined to pouring things from a bottle into a glass.

I do not want to give the impression that we were a group of perambulating alcoholics, but after a day on the road it is pleasant to settle into a comfortable chair before dinner, look out over the lake or mountains or whatever it is that Nature provides for the traveler's enjoyment at that point, and sip something besides chilled sherry.

Whiskey is so scarce, and so expensive in consequence, that we concentrated on Martinis. Unfortunately the Scandinavian idea of a Martini is a concoction composed of four-fifths warm sweet vermouth and one-fifth sweet Danish gin. Each time we explained carefully, first to the owner of the hotel, then to the bartender, and finally to anybody who would listen, that we wanted our cocktails made from four parts dry English gin and one part dry vermouth, shaken until ice-cold. Everyone understood completely. We exchanged countless bows on the subject—but the results were almost always the same—four-fifths sweet warm vermouth and one-fifth sweet Danish gin.

The Åregården Hotel presented an exception. They mixed our cocktails according to instructions and with the care of an apothecary. Unfortunately for us, however, they kept their liquor supply in a deep freeze. This saved them much trouble cracking ice, but almost ruined us.

Down in the valley below the hotel was a tiny church of obvious antiquity, even in a country which specialized in old churches. To enter the churchyard one passed through a pagoda-like structure of stone and brown, carved wood which housed the church bell. This was our first introduction to detached belfries, which are to Sweden what the windmill is to Holland.

We walked down the road before dinner to inspect it. The old church was locked. While we were peering through the windows, four workmen came across the field, their rakes on their shoulders. They sat down on a bench outside the belfry and waited until six o'clock. Then one of them pulled the bell rope nine times with long intervals between each pull, during which he leaned on the rope and chatted with his friends. It was a kind of Swedish Angelus.

While we were finishing dinner, the lady manager of the hotel told us that there was a young man waiting for us who wished to act as a guide in showing us the church. She explained that he had brought a friend who helped in such matters because of language difficulties.

We did not particularly want a guide and we had already seen the church. At the moment it seemed to us that the sensible thing would be to go to bed immediately after dinner, but we were always fearful of creating an international incident by some failure in courtesy, so, when we had finished, we joined the young men at the entrance. Everyone bowed and we set out for our second visit to the church, rather puzzled about the helper as both spoke English fluently.

They unlocked it. We examined it carefully. They locked it up again. They took our pictures from various angles with professional-looking cameras. We began to get set for a large fee. When we returned to the hotel I asked, somewhat apprehensively, what the charge for their services as guides and photographers might be.

They both seemed dismayed at the question. The leader gave me his card which indicated that he operated a photo and tourist service. I had apparently hurt his feelings deeply by the suggestion that he was to take payment. He said that he would send us copies of the photographs and that they would be with his compliments.

The name of this remarkable young man is Åke Sundström. I hope that any readers of this book may find occasion to do some business with Åke (and his efficient helper) on a more professional basis and thus repay our obligation for their courtesy.

We slept that night between sheets and under two big, red blankets. It was cold in that mountain village. The elusive *dyne* had disappeared at the Swedish border. It was nice to have bedding under which one could roll around without feet popping out or without tossing everything onto the floor.

12

Sundsvall

THE FOLLOWING MORNING WE SET OUT FOR SUNDSVALL through a country of lakes and fir trees and red and white houses with red-tiled roofs; a country of broad fields and slat fences and white cows with black ears.

It was a beautiful blue-sky day with fat, white clouds floating over the dark evergreen forests and the tidy farms and the log-strewn surfaces of the lakes. There is nothing gradual about the transition from Norway to Sweden. One passes instantly from the untamed to the cultivated, from the savage to the bucolic, from a bugle serenade to chamber music.

Lucy and Sara are self-declared sentimentalists. They are the kind of women who go mad, on the one hand, about tiny infants and newborn animals. And at the other end of the scale, natural grandeur reduces them to tears and a five-thousand-foot drop fills them with reverent awe.

Naturally enough, therefore, they had fallen completely in love with Norway, its miniature farms, its tiny buildings, its yellow ponies, and its enormous scenery. The smallness of the things that man had made and the largeness of Nature's handiwork had struck responsive chords in their breasts.

Being women of strong loyalties, they were not prepared to switch their allegiances easily and they entered Sweden as a girl would leave a lover for a blind date—prepared to take it out on the new for having deprived them of the old.

East of Lake Storsjön and Östersund we entered the forest

again—a forest which apparently went on forever. For mile after mile the road wound along the bottom of a green slot. We had eaten early. It was now two o'clock and everyone was growing hungry and rather cross. Finding a picnic place in this trackless Swedish woodland was not an easy matter.

Just as we were preparing to stop and eat lunch in the middle of the road, Nature relented and provided a lovely, forest-bordered lake. We sat on a pile of bark-peeled logs and ate our usual bread-and-cheese, bread-and-marmalade combination, topped off by oranges which Sara had bought in Åre and which turned out to be dwarf grapefruits. George became impressed with the color possibilities of grapefruit peelings against peeled logs and used half a roll of film taking snapshots of them.

Food does wonders with a woman's heart. Sara and Lucy were happy for the first time since entering Sweden. They looked out on the countryside with new and friendly eyes, particularly when the road burst out of the forest and met the beautiful Indalsälven, flowing down to the sea between fir-covered hills.

It was a brilliant, green valley dotted with red farm buildings and hydroelectric plants and streaked with hay driers which became larger and larger as we neared the sea until they swelled into gigantic affairs rising to a height of thirty feet. Just how they put the hay on the top bar is the secret of the Swedes.

Sundsvall is an industrial town ringed with pulp mills. In the center is the Knaust Hotel, a huge old caravansary, its lobby dominated by a broad marble staircase which splits halfway up and goes off in opposite directions. It is the kind of a staircase that musical-comedy directors like to introduce in the finale of the last act for storing the surplus members of the cast.

Unfortunately there was no cast grouped on the stairs when we arrived. In fact the only person in sight was the porter behind the desk, a dour-looking man who took a strong dislike to me at first sight.

I explained with the overpoliteness of the helpless that we had made our reservations weeks before. He pulled an old shoe box from under the desk and rumpled through an assortment of what must have once been letters. There were no reservations.

Under such circumstances there is nothing to do but keep leaning on the desk, saying the same thing over and over. After a while the porter became bored and obviously welcomed interruptions.

The first presented itself in the form of a little girl who handed him a silver krona. He took it and put it in the till. A few moments later the little girl returned accompanied by an angry Swede. One did not have to understand Swedish to follow the ensuing conversation. After a few minutes, the porter opened the till and gave the krona back. Sensing a defeat, I followed up with a new and vigorous attack.

An Englishman came up to the desk and said that he had reservations. The porter could find none. The Englishman became savagely abusive. It was like a scene from *Uncle Tom's Cabin*. The porter found the reservation. "That's the only way to get anything out of these chaps," said the Englishman cheerily as he turned away. I immediately became abusive. The porter rumpled once more through the pile of letters, but apparently I lacked technique, for he found nothing.

A young Swede approached and whispered in the porter's ear. To my surprise the latter laughed audibly and whispered back to the young man. While they were exchanging boyish confidences, George came up to the desk, picked up a notebook which he found lying under some travel folders, and almost immediately located our reservations—which had been scratched out.

Ordinarily, George is a meek man. He apparently places a high value on shelter, however, for now he became a veritable lion.

He roared at the porter, shook the book at him and the fellow melted like ice on a stove. George has English blood in him, which may be significant. Lucy and Sara were given an ordinary double room and George and I were given what the porter called special quarters—which described them admirably.

The dining room at the Knaust is an enormous, red affair. At one end an orchestra was playing bad Viennese. The headwaiter looked like Rudy Vallee, which was unfortunate, for it was the direct cause of our sitting in that room for three hours and spending large sums of money.

Like a headwaiter on a French ocean liner, Mr. Vallee indicated that there was nothing fit to eat on the menu and suggested the *spécialité de la maison*, which he said was salmon boiled in paper. While we were waiting for that, he said that the chef could throw together a mushroom soup which he thought might please persons of our obvious caliber. Lucy and Sara become like molding clay under this kind of treatment. Without consulting us further, they gave Rudy a full power of attorney.

The soup arrived in an enormous china container which looked suspiciously like those articles that one used to find under beds in country hotels. It was borne in by a waiter in the triumphal manner of a medieval page carrying in the boar's head. The other guests, some of whom did not recognize it as a soup tureen, began to sit up and take notice.

About an hour later the salmon arrived, sewn into a huge bag of greasy brown paper. A special serving table was brought in. With a flourish, Mr. Vallee slit the paper with a carving knife. An odor came from its interior reminiscent of a steam bath I used to patronize in a gymnasium on 44th Street. The other guests knew definitely that something out of the ordinary was going on. Everyone craned to look. Those in the back of the room stood up. The house detective, who was seated at a small table in the corner, began to give us his undivided attention.

Mr. Vallee informed us that he only had one dessert which was suitable for a meal such as this. It was fresh, wild strawberries. Without waiting for a reply, he departed and about an hour later three waiters entered, one behind the other. The leader bore proudly an enormous bowl containing hundreds and hundreds of sour little berries. Protruding from them at all angles were large napkins rolled into cones.

I have forgotten what the other two waiters bore. I think one carried the sugar and the other the cream. The room was really agog now. Some of the guests visibly restrained themselves from shouting and even the house detective smiled wearily.

It was almost eleven o'clock. We gave all our money to Rudy and staggered out into the black streets for air.

13

To Rättvik
Via Gävle

FROM SUNDSVALL IT WAS AN UNEVENTFUL RUN DOWN THE coast to Gävle.

Distant places, like the Gulf of Bothnia, are apt to become tinged with romance. As is so often the case, however, when we finally met it face to face we found it disappointingly like the offshore waters of Connecticut and Rhode Island as glimpsed from the windows of the New York, New Haven and Hartford.

Could we have agreed on where to eat our picnic lunch, there would have been no problems at all to keep us awake. Somehow in Norway this matter had never presented any difficulties. There it was either raining and we were forced to eat in the car, or we chose the first level place we came to, which usually commanded such a superlative view that no one could think up a good reason to disagree.

In Sweden, however, it apparently never rained, the weather was made for picnicking and available places were an öre a dozen. As a result it was impossible to agree on any one.

For example, here we were within two miles of the Swedish coast line. What more natural or desirable than to seek some charming headland and make faces at the Russians while we munched our bread and cheese?

George and I happened to be occupying the front seat and so, whenever we saw a likely-looking side road leading toward the water, we left the highway and followed it. Unfortunately these ventures all ended in farmyards where we were obliged to turn around with difficulty and retreat under the hostile eyes of the farmer and his entire family.

Sara and Lucy have a Chinese sense of face coupled with exaggerated ideas about the sacredness of private property. When several of these side trips had ended in the same way, they prohibited further experiments. As a result, after ten miles of argument, we ended up in the corner of a shadeless field beside the main road.

One would have thought that, having spent an hour arguing about the best place to eat a sandwich, we could have settled for one that did not contain a bull, or, looking at the matter from another angle, that we might have discovered the presence of such an undesirable element before establishing ourselves in the corner furthest from the road and spreading our luncheon materials all over the grass.

The bull, who was apparently more alert than we were about such things, had been observing us from the beginning with much interest and now began a slow stalk across the field while we started a check on the barbed wire fence behind us.

At that particular moment, a cow came strolling down the highway. It was an unusual thing for a cow to be doing, but this was Sweden and there she was. She stopped, surveyed the bull across the fence and gave vent to a series of heartbreaking moos. Then she continued her walk. It was an extremely feminine gambit.

The bull, quite obviously, did his best to resist this kind of sirenism. He lowered his head, pawed the ground, turned his back to her, and made vulgar noises. Then he gave in, found a hole in the fence, and followed her slowly down the road. We finished our lunch much relieved.

This incident is only mentioned to substantiate our initial state-

ment that from Sundsvall it was an uneventful run down the coast
to Gävle.

Gävle would have looked good to us even if we had never seen
Sundsvall. It was a city of shaded parks and tree-lined streets
with a tree-bordered stream dividing the main thoroughfare.

We stopped to ask a workman the direction to the Grand Hotel.
He lifted his cap politely, got on his bicycle and pedaled before
us for three blocks to the entrance to the hotel. There he lifted his
cap again and pedaled back from whence he had come without
having spoken a word or accepted an öre for his courtesy. Had the
Gävle Chamber of Commerce planned it, they could not have done
a better job.

There is nothing about Gävle in the guidebooks, but there should
be. And there should be something about the Grand Hotel, for
it is new and luxurious and its dining room overlooks a tree-shaded
court with a fountain playing in the center. It was just what we
needed at that particular point.

We walked about the town before dinner. Sara and Lucy became
unaccountably fascinated by the municipal firehouse, a great brown-
stone castle with bright red fire apparatus gleaming through the
arched doorways. They are not the kind of girls who hang around
firehouses at home but they seemed unable to tear themselves
away from this one.

A blond young man came out of the firehouse, bowed and
asked if we would care to inspect the vehicles. He showed us everything in minute detail. In a moment he would have had the hose
out, playing it up and down the street for our instruction. On the
driver's seat of the hook-and-ladder Lucy, who never fails to note
an article of human apparel, male or female, spotted a pair of
white spiked running shoes.

"Are you a runner?" she asked in her best conversational manner.

"Ah, yes," he said, "I run very frequently in your Madison Square Garden."

The fire helmets hung in a neat row on the wall, their polished brass gleaming. Across the square, in front of the railroad station, little locomotives, striped with glistening brass, puffed up and down, emitting shrill squeals. In a park beside the tracks, hundreds and hundreds of bicycles slanted in neat rows from their racks. White-coated stationmasters ran aimlessly up and down the graveled platform beside the railroad tracks, tooting on flutelike whistles.

From an immaculate dock, we watched a lumber boat being towed out into the channel by a toy tug. Its brass was, of course, glistening in the evening sun. A man on a bicycle with a child in a seat strapped to the handle bars and another over the rear wheel, watched the boat's departure and then rode slowly away.

Dozens of small sailboats, tethered side by side in a nearby slip, bobbed up and down in the wash from some unseen vessel. In the canal, which ran down the main street, shiny motorboats waited for their owners to call it a day and go home. A woman passed on a bicycle; a basket seat strapped to her handle bars contained a large collie dog, its front paws carefully tucked into two wicker pockets over the front wheel.

We dined looking down into the courtyard with the flowers and the fountain. A Hungarian orchestra in red jackets and an endless repertoire of sentimental airs, caused Lucy and Sara to become immediately emotional. As the evening wore on they were constantly on the verge of tears. There was a neat little bar in one corner manned by an English bartender who claimed to know all about American drinks. I ordered a bourbon old-fashioned. He produced a double-Martini glass filled with warm Scotch with a thimble of ice bobbing around in the middle of it. It was the fly that made the ointment perfect.

Across the courtyard, two young men spent the period from

seven until midnight sipping a brown liquid from champagne glasses and ended the evening in fits of hysterical laughter. They were still laughing when we went to bed, filled with enthusiasm for Gävle and the Grand Hotel.

On the following day we drove to Rättvik on the shores of Lake Siljan which the Swedish guidebooks like to call the "blue eye of Dalarna."

Months before when we had started to plan the trip, Sara and Lucy had sat in on all conferences. They are both somewhat allergic to maps, however, and as a result whenever they were present, the conversation always seemed to drift from the question of where we would stop and how we would get there to a discussion of someone who was about to have a baby in Detroit, Michigan— or a dress that one of them had seen in a little shop on Madison Avenue.

As time went on they both tended to leave the details to George and me. This made things simpler and we accepted the arrangement willingly although without foresight. It was not until we arrived in Norway that we realized it might have drawbacks as well as advantages.

For as the trip progressed, Lucy and Sara, being two very normal women, became increasingly sick and tired of being led around by their good-looking noses from one strange place to another without having any say in the matter whatsoever. The fact that they had voluntarily relinquished their vote months before did not enter into their reasoning.

As a result the approach to any new place involved a period of great nervous strain for George and me as Sara and Lucy automatically took the attitude that they were being dragged into a rathole. They assumed, moreover, that this spot, which we had so unaccountably chosen, was surrounded by places of known charm and world-wide reputation which only a couple of morons would have passed up.

Their disapproval was, of course, merely an instinctive attempt to re-establish their individuality and their natural rights of self-assertion. But even if this had been clearer to us, it would not have helped much at the moment.

The guidebooks and the publicity pamphlets were also partly to blame. In this instance, for example, they had played up Lake Siljan and Rättvik to such a degree that anyone who had ever traveled beyond the city limits of his home town would know that they could not make good. The result was that when Lake Siljan, "the blue eye of Dalarna," hove in sight and proved to be a large body of water, more gray at the moment than blue, its far shores almost hidden in a heat mist, George and I knew immediately that we were licked.

Sara and Lucy took up the scent like a pair of beagles and were off in full cry. As we reached the shore some miles south of Rättvik they discovered a number of summer cottages which had the tired look of inexpensive summer cottages throughout the world. They declared that it was just what they had anticipated. Lucy said with great bitterness that it reminded her of Lake Winnepesaukee, and Sara agreed. I do not know why they chose Winnepesaukee as their basic low point. I had always thought it a beautiful place.

Then we came to the village. We were now in the heart of the "costume belt" where "the country folk still cling proudly to their colorful native dress." Rättvik's single street was lined with souvenir stores and postcard shops. The only people in costumes were the tourists who wandered aimlessly about in odd-looking slacks selecting postal cards of country folk clinging proudly to their colorful native dress.

Sara and Lucy gave a whoop of sadistic joy and settled down to hate everything, with George and myself tying for first honors.

The famous hotel Siljansborg is set far up the side of the hill overlooking the lake. It is a beautifully appointed, lovely spot owned and managed by a remarkable and charming young woman by the name of Britt Arpi.

We sat on the broad, flagstoned terrace after dinner watching the sun's afterglow on a huge cloud far away to the west. Sara and Lucy had slept, they had walked together down a path of their own discovery to the edge of the lake, they had stumbled on a historic church and picked up a yellow dog. In addition to these satisfying experiences they had eaten an excellent dinner preceded by flawless Martinis.

"I can't bear to think we're only going to be here two days," said Sara.

"I don't see why we couldn't shift things around," said Lucy, "and cut out some of those dumps you're taking us to after we leave here."

There are certain aspects of a woman's character that seem devoid of shame, guilt, or remorse.

14

Dalarna

THE ANCIENT, TREE-SHADED CHURCH AT RÄTTVIK, STANDING
on a rise of ground by the shore of Lake Siljan, dominates the
countryside as it has dominated the lives of its inhabitants for hundreds of years. Each Sunday its square, dome-capped tower becomes
a hub toward which the community converges by paths and roads
and water—and so strong is the power of tradition that on this day
many still wear their colorful local costumes just as the guidebooks
promise.

Rättvik is a charming place in which to be on a fair Sunday
summer morning, and it must have been an even more exciting one
a generation ago before the publicity sirens had started to wail and
the gasoline motor had destroyed its remoteness. Then it was not
"a costume belt," but a community of simple, hard-working people
who wore their native dress as naturally and as proudly as the women
of New York wear their mink and the cattle men of Montana their
broad-brimmed hats.

Whether the old costumes have survived because of, or in spite of,
the curious crowds who flock to see them, only time will tell. Whatever integrity they represent, however, can scarcely retain its footing
much longer against the force of a thousand camera lenses.

Even though the worshipers may eventually abandon the old tradition rather than put on a free vaudeville show for the summer
trade, the old church itself will never compromise. Inside, the wall
paintings of dying martyrs and the incongruous jumble of saints
and gnomes and little animals are just as available for the diversion

of those who become bored with the sermon as they were five hundred years ago.

Outside, the thick walls gleam white in the brilliant sunshine and cast their shadow on a neat little graveyard. Each grave has a headstone which forms one end of a minute, stone-bordered enclosure. Inside its narrow boundaries no blade of grass is allowed to grow, and the sandy soil is worked by the survivors into intricate geometric patterns with the aid of small wooden rakes. There seems to be a morbid competition in this matter, for we never saw a Swedish graveyard in which someone was not striving industriously to devise more original patterns than his neighbor.

Below the church, clustered at the edge of the lake, is a group of log huts. These were at one time for the horses of the worshipers, for it can be cold in these latitudes and the Lutheran service can be long. Now they are merely souvenirs of a picturesque past, having long since been supplanted by alcohol in the radiator.

As we were standing in the churchyard admiring the entrance, a motherly-looking woman in peasant costume came out and stood on the top step looking dreamily out over the lake. She wore an embroidered linen blouse with a green-bodice affair over it, and a black skirt with a panel in the front like an apron, striped horizontally in red, green, and white.

Clara Laughlin, in her book *So You're Going to Scandinavia,* had warned us earnestly about taking pictures of the natives in costume unless we first obtained permission, but this was too much for us. We took three pictures simultaneously. Her eyes came down from the distant shores of the lake and lost their dreamy look. She asked us a sharp question in Swedish and our hearts were filled with dismay. Clearly, we had committed that gross breach of good manners which we had been dreading ever since we arrived in Oslo. We had done harm to the reputation of our country.

We tried to apologize in that queer kind of broken English to which Americans resort when talking to someone who does not understand any English at all. The woman only stared at us coldly and repeated her question. After a hurried conference we delegated George to approach her with gold, but this gesture of bad taste only added fuel to the fire. She waved it aside imperiously and repeated her question in Swedish.

A man in a tweed suit, several sizes too small for him, entered the churchyard. To our relief we found that he spoke English. We explained the humiliating position in which we had so stupidly placed ourselves and asked him to intercede in our behalf.

He spoke to the woman briefly. "She only wanted to make sure," he said, "that the pictures you took of her are in color."

Shortly after noon we set off for Mora and the Zorn Museum at the head of the lake, carrying a picnic lunch and minute instructions from Miss Arpi as to where to eat it most dramatically. She directed us by back roads to a little church near Mora which she particularly wanted us to explore. We were then to go to a spot nearby where we could enjoy our lunch on the highest point of ground around the lake.

It was late. Our back-road route was longer than we had anticipated. Lucy and Sara were hungry and I had noticed on previous occasions that under these conditions they lost all feeling for vagabondism, exploration, or the picturesque. Sara drove the last part of the journey, wheeling around the corners at sixty miles an hour and coming to a screaming stop where a narrow lane led up a hill to Miss Arpi's church.

It was a lovely old building, standing in a grove of trees and overlooking miles of rolling woodland. At the suggestion that we stop and explore it a bit, Lucy and Sara snorted contemptuously.

"Why should we?" they asked in the imperious way of women who have fixed their minds on other goals. "We know what is in it."

Stockholm is one of the beautiful cities of the world. (*Swedish National Travel Office*)

To be sure of a front room in Stockholm's Grand, one should apply at birth. (*Swedish National Travel Office*)

Swift, silent traffic which seems to glide through the streets. (*Swedish National Travel Office*)

Old Stockholm where even the summer sun rarely gets below the second floor. (*Swedish National Travel Office*)

New Stockholm where the sun worshipers gather in the squares at noon. (*Swedish National Travel Office*)

The Swedes like detached belfries   The phone booths are semiprivate

The walls of Visby are crumbling here and there, but that is the right of any wall after a thousand years. (*Swedish National Travel Office*)

The old church at Rättvik stands at a crossroads in a changing world

It's a pleasant place to be on Sunday

Scandinavia belongs to the sea and the sea to
Scandinavia. (*Swedish National Travel Office*)

The endless flow of Sweden's forests moves like a glacier
toward the sea. (*Swedish National Travel Office*)

Be it a peasant's farmhouse or a king's palace, the Swedes have always liked to touch things up a bit. (*Swedish National Travel Office*)

The dirt road wound on up the hill. We followed it to a spot near the top, commanding a view of the great valleys to the north.

"Here it is," cried George. "The high point!" Sara was still driving. "It isn't," she said somewhat rudely, and followed the lane into a dense wood where it gradually became a trail and eventually ended at a mossy, padlocked gate. We turned the car around with difficulty, getting stuck twice in the soft mold on either side. Lucy and Sara declared that it was very stupid of George and me to get into such a place, and that they were going to eat right here in view of the fact that neither of us appeared to know what we were doing.

There are moments when it isn't wise to argue. We munched our sandwiches in the green half-light of the forest. As a matter of fact, we had seen so many views that it was pleasant to see nothing but a world of moss and leaves connected by green-brown tree trunks.

As we were preparing to depart, an old woman suddenly appeared from nowhere. The gate was still locked, but there she was plodding down the road ahead of our parked car. It was that kind of a place.

George decided, very sensibly, that she was a witch and in order to eliminate any possibility of charms, enchantments, or other forms of thaumaturgy, he thought it would be prudent to invite her to ride with us. It was obviously the first time in her hundred and more years of life that she had ever ridden in an automobile. Before we had shifted out of low gear she was seized with a fit of giggles, and as we let her out near the main road fifteen minutes later she was still laughing.

When we looked back, she had disappeared. Lucy said that she had gone around the corner of a nearby farmhouse. George and I said nothing.

Mora is the home village of the late Anders Zorn. It was there that he did the etchings for which he is best known to most Americans; but in a modern museum which houses a large collection of his work are also many examples of his remarkable water colors and portraits in oil.

I make no pretense of being informed on the subject of art, but I know that what we saw that afternoon under the friendly and able guidance of the assistant curator, Mr. Forstman, caused us to come away with a sense of having discovered something both beautiful and important.

That was one aspect of our visit—the nobler aspect. The other was that museums or, indeed, guided tours of any sort, have a tendency to give Lucy and Sara what is technically known as macaroni knees. At home, when I am forced, on rare occasions, to go shopping with Lucy, she will push her way through the crowded aisles of one store after another for hours at a time without showing any signs of fatigue, while I find myself staggering like a young calf and struggling to resist the impulse to sit down on escalators.

It seems to be part of the basic difference between men and women. Possibly there are economic roots at the bottom of it all, for it may well be that women are fatigued by the sight of things which cannot be bought, and men by those which can.

Whatever the cause, Lucy and Sara staggered forth from Mr. Zorn's studio like desert travelers who have given their all and can go no further. Next to the studio was a beautiful old church which had been highly recommended to us by somebody. Their reaction to the idea of setting foot within its time-stained doors was so violent that we went back to the car and returned somewhat silently to Rättvik by the shore road.

Around us moved the Saturday afternoon life of Dalarna; athletic young men on bicycles, stripped to the waist; men on half-size motorcycles, dressed from head to foot in helmets, goggles and rubber suits, crouched over their handle bars as they tore along at a cool thirty miles an hour; on our left a little railroad train, a light, delicate affair with the familiar pressure-cooker whistle. The engineer waved to us gaily and an official in a white coat saluted smartly from the rear platform. There was a carnival atmosphere in the air.

George, who is an indefatigable bolsterer of sagging morale, launched into a colorful discussion of Dalarna based on years of no research whatsoever. Dalarna, he declared, was beautiful and pleasing for the reason that everything in it was functional and had been handed down unchanged from one generation to another because it best served the purpose for which it was designed.

Not having been interrupted by either Sara or Lucy up to this point, he became enthusiastic and began to develop his idea. It was the kind of a conversation that Boswell was always reporting in his journal. All true beauty, George said, had to undergo the test of time and utility. The thing which endures because it serves a purpose gradually acquires harmonious form and by the same token, the ugliness of our present world is due to the fact that we have untied ourselves from the past. As a consequence our modern forms, instead of developing naturally, must be created synthetically overnight.

It was an excellent effort and the silent attention with which it was received by the rear seat was a tribute to its merit. George prepared to go on. I looked in the rear-view mirror. Lucy and Sara were asleep.

Life around Lake Siljan comes to a sharp focus on Sunday. Early Sunday morning, Miss Arpi drove with us to the south end of the lake where, at Leksand, we might see the people of that community entering their church after which we would have time to return and watch the people of Rättvik coming out of theirs.

The great white church at Leksand is approached along a broad avenue bordered by giant birch trees. As we arrived, two funeral processions came around the corner and lined up between the birches preparatory to entering the graveyard. One was that of an adult. The coffin was borne on poles by eight men. The other group was headed by a tiny white casket carried by six men. The mourners followed each coffin dressed in their local costumes, the women wearing the yellow apron of mourning.

A single deep-noted bell began to toll slowly in the great, timbered belfry behind us. Its note was so deep that one could feel its vibrations run up and down the spine. The two funeral processions moved slowly toward the cemetery gateway, led by a dignitary in a long black coat and followed by the minister in black knee britches.

Then suddenly, all the bells in the belfry let go—the large and the small. The little ones were glad and hopeful. They spoke of youth and spring and living things, but through their eager confusion the steady boom of the great bass bell told of the inevitable end.

The costumed natives crowded into church. We took pictures and drove back to Rättvik. There the costumed natives crowded out of church. We took pictures and drove to the hotel for lunch.

Late that afternoon we went again to the old church at Rättvik to hear a choir of a hundred voices trained and directed by Hugo Alfven, director of music at Uppsala University. The participants were all local country people and here all were dressed in their native costumes. For the first time the costumes suddenly became an integral part of the surroundings. There was no longer any question of whether they were worn because of, or in spite of, the tourists. This was the real, the preinvasion, Dalarna. Here were the integrity and the cohesion for which we had sought. The singers seemed to sense it and sang with a full-throated enthusiasm which conveyed itself to the audience.

15

To Stockholm
Via Uppsala

WE LEFT RÄTTVIK WITH A REGRET WHICH MORE THAN offset the hostility with which we had entered it two days before. Sara and Lucy made no attempt to hide their displeasure at being dragged away from such a desirable place, and their comments on Uppsala and Stockholm which lay immediately ahead boded no good to George and me.

We were headed southeast. The rugged mountains and the great forests lay behind us, and we were coasting down invisible slopes to the sea through the rich farm and industrial areas which give Sweden the appearance, at least, of one of the most prosperous countries in the world.

It was a colorful, ever-shifting scene—fertile fields—huge barns —red houses with vertical clapboards—bicycles all over the road, making speed impossible—squat little motorcycles giving forth a liquid purr—vacationists with bulging back packs—long rows of modern, barrack-like apartment buildings—birch-bordered roadsides—and great trucks which thundered murderously down the middle of the highway. We were getting bolder and no longer gave way to them. At the last moment they always went over where they belonged—which was very fortunate.

We lunched in Sala at the Stadshotell. It was a charming little place with a glass-protected porch where one could eat and look out over a garden badly in need of weeding.

The waitress, wearing the white shirtwaist and black skirt which seems to be the national costume for waitresses in Sweden, presented us with a bill of fare printed in Swedish and stood with pencil and pad poised. She was a pleasure to behold, but of no practical help whatsoever.

A blue-eyed girl, lunching at the next table, saw our difficulty and came to our rescue. We asked her if it would be possible to get some kind of cold soup and an entree. She gave instructions to the waitress which she assured us would result in a cold soup of merit and a type of Swedish steak which she thought we would find delicious.

This cheered us up immediately and George and I consumed several bottles of beer in anticipation. As usual, we had plenty of time. About forty-five minutes later we received four bowls of junket blanketed with sour cream followed by four tattered bits of leather masquerading under an excellent sauce.

George demanded water. As I have mentioned before he was a great water drinker. He liked to start a meal by dashing down a tumbler or two and every few minutes thereafter he would send another half-glass on its way, topping off with a veritable deluge.

In Scandinavia, however, this is regarded as a highly unconventional procedure and no hotel will aid or abet it without a struggle. To request a glass of water is to tread on soft ground. If you are urgent enough, it will be brought to you as it would to anyone in distress. The waiter will usually hover about, however, and if you do not drink it quickly, he will snatch it away and disappear. Clearly it is not the kind of stuff they like to leave lying around.

It was a situation which always irritated George profoundly. "Leave that glass alone," he would roar, as the waiter tried to remove it, "Leave it here and bring me a *pitcher* of water." And then he would add, somewhat triumphantly, "We are Americans." This last statement always puzzled the waiter. I think George did it to throw him off balance. He would talk to the headwaiter and they would cast glances at our table. Sometimes they would even bring the pitcher of water, but after a few minutes they usually thought better of their decision and took it away again.

Months before we had reserved rooms at the Hotel Gillet in Uppsala, but the moment I laid eyes on the porter my instinct told me that we were in for trouble.

He had a cold, masklike face which had probably never broken into a smile since the day he was born. It was a face which combined the characteristics of a drill sergeant and a baseball umpire. Yes, he said cryptically, our name was on the blotter, but our accommodations had not been confirmed. There had never been any rooms available and there were none now. It was quite evident that, for all of him, we might bed down in the lovely old stream which ran down the middle of the main street just outside.

Finally, after we had threatened him with everything from lawsuit to mayhem, he made several telephone calls one of which eventually brought us to a tired little hostelry near the railroad tracks. It must have been part of some Swedish Youth Movement, for the management seemed to be in the hands of two little boys. They were the only human beings we saw from the time we arrived until we left the following noon. They carried our bags up to our rooms and they carried them down again. They made out our bill, and they answered our questions—mostly inaccurately. They were nice boys, but it was not a good hotel nor was it a propitious way to enter a city. Lucy and Sara treated George and myself with the cold politeness that they reserved for incompetents and doormen who could not get them taxis.

Sydney Clark says about this charming city: "Uppsala is one of the world's little giants of history and of culture and its myriad strands of achievement give it a voice of character rarely matched by any city in any country." That is pretty strong talk, but it is just about the situation. Uppsala is a city of enormous antiquity, great cultural background and so cluttered with historic "musts" that it was a bit of arrogance on our part to allot a half day to it.

We visited the cathedral that evening before dinner. Like cathedrals everywhere, it is still in process of building after four or five hundred years. As we entered, the interior was filled with the reverberations of a kind of antiphonal chant which came first from one side, then the other. It reminded us of Italian cathedrals. And then we remembered that Sweden is a Lutheran country. It was puzzling until we discovered that the sound proceeded from two guides shouting competitive descriptions of the interior to their little flocks of Swedish tourists.

The Castle of Uppsala, a dusky-pink un-castle-like building, sat on a hill overlooking the city. It was so covered with scaffolding that we thought it was just being built until we learned from the books that it was several hundred years old. In a separate belfry nearby hung a great bell which is rung at six each morning and at nine in the evening. These are the hours that the students at the university must devote to their studies. At least that was the opinion of a good Swedish queen who died in 1588. She left a trust fund to insure its being rung at those hours in perpetuity. I tried to find out who the trustees were. They must have been excellent investors, for the bell is still being rung.

That night we dined at Flustret, a garden café beside a pond where a flock of swans performed a ghostly patrol up and down the quiet water. To offset the unpleasant things which have been said about Scandinavian Martinis, let me record that at Flustret the thirsty traveler will get a faultless one.

A fountain played with a rubber ball. In the corner, a child was crying. At the next table a man with a huge mustache was making love to a blonde in a huge hat. We ate a leisurely, delicious dinner, speculating, among other things, on the men who are always to be found in restaurants like Flustret, staring into space over a small drink and who are there when one leaves several hours later, still staring into space and with the same drink in front of them.

For once, it did not infuriate us that it took almost three hours to eat. We walked home through the dark shadows of the trees which bordered the old canal, watching the Maxfield Parrish afterglow in the topaz sky and feeling more kindly toward Uppsala.

On the following morning we pocketed our pride and breakfasted at the Hotel Gillet. The porter, instead of hanging his head in shame, bowed deeply and dared to express the hope that we had had a pleasant night.

We had four hours to see Uppsala. After spending one of them at the Gillet arguing about what we should visit and what we should leave out, we hired a young law student to show us around. It was just as well we did. He left us at Flustret at half-past twelve, limp with exhaustion—and we had only scratched the surface.

With a fine sense of chronological fitness, he started at Gamla Uppsala (Old Uppsala) with its great burial mounds where the old-timers are reported to have made human sacrifices and the foundation of a viking temple may be seen through a hole in the floor of an eighteenth-century church. As we came out, a flight of army jet planes thundered past, flying low.

We visited Uppsala's new co-operative apartments. We gaped in admiring wonder at the beautiful central building of the university. We revisited the cathedral. At the library we inspected the illuminated manuscripts. It was there that Sara and Lucy went on strike. They declared they would not be dragged to one more museum, disregarding the fact that we had visited none that day. They refused, in fact, to see another sight of any kind and sat moodily in the car while George and I paid our superficial respects to the castle and the university. At that point we also threw up the sponge, said good-by to our guide, staggered to Flustret and—you have guessed it—ordered double Martinis.

It was late and we wanted to push on to Stockholm. Knowing the time required to acquire a meal in a Scandinavian restaurant, we had a preliminary consultation with the headwaiter, explaining to him that we were in great haste. He assured us that we would be out before one could say "Skål."

We ordered something that he said was not only a quick dish but would also turn out to be the corned beef hash with egg of which Americans were so fond. We did not want corned beef hash, but it is wrong to dampen such rare enthusiasm—and besides we were in a hurry. Eventually a great platter was placed before us on which sliced boiled potatoes and sliced meat were arranged in alternate layers with four medium-boiled eggs, their shells removed, arranged conveniently around the edges. These we shattered over the sliced meat and potatoes and presto—corned beef hash with egg!

We had left our car outside the Gillet and our cameras with the porter. He handed them to us now with Chesterfieldian politeness. "So glad," he said, "we had you here. We hope you will come again."

It was the kind of a remark that creates apoplectics. When the swelling in our necks had subsided, we explained to him with some frankness that he had *not* had us there, that we had slept in a panther's den as a result, and that we would *not* come back. He looked quite blank. "So glad," he said with unruffled urbanity, "we had you here. Do come again."

It is only forty miles from Uppsala to Stockholm. We knew we were nearing the city when we picked up a two-lane bicycle path and then a trolley line whose blue cars appeared to roll on rubber rails, each pulling two other Silent Sams behind it.

We had dreaded this entrance into a strange city while still jittery about driving on the left-hand side. Had we known how bad it was actually going to be, however, we would probably have settled down permanently at the Boys' Hotel in Uppsala.

It was about four-thirty in the afternoon, when the rising tide of bicycles, bearing their owners home from their daily toil, was reaching its crest. As we came nearer to the center of things, the cycle paths spilled their traffic into the street and disappeared. Once more we found ourselves traveling down a river of bicycles, as a boat moves through water. Their back wheels were only an inch or two ahead of our front bumper and our fenders brushed against them on either side.

Apparently, however, we, who had four wheels under us, were the only ones who were disturbed by all this. The cyclists rode stolidly and unconcernedly ahead. Occasionally one would fling out his arm and, without a sidewise glance, cut across our bow and then across a wave of oncoming bicycles and trucks, but somehow or other metal never connected with flesh.

A new problem immediately arose. Quite obviously we did not know where we were going, and in this living stream it was impossible to stop and ask anyone even if they could have understood us. Something had to be done, however, and after a long struggle we managed to drift over to the curb as a swimmer in a swift current will work his way to shore. A policeman stood beneath a tree looking bored. When he saw us his face lighted up and he proceeded to give us directions, so complicated as to be completely unintelligible. The only thing that we understood was his gloved hand, which pointed to the right.

We were entering a large plaza with streets radiating from it star-fashion in all directions. Trolley cars were crossing and crisscrossing. Great trucks were bumping along without regard for human life and everywhere, in the intervening spaces, were bicycles.

There was no temporizing with such a situation. Shutting our eyes, we turned sharp right across the plaza—sharp right in front of the bicycles—sharp right in front of the trolley cars and trucks. There was a squealing of brakes. Foreign words rang out. Somewhere a whistle blew. It sounded as if it might have been blown by a policeman.

We stepped on the gas and darted into one of the radiating streets only to find that it was a one-way affair—and, as was to have been expected, it was going the wrong way. This was no time for weak vacillation, however. We kept right on to the end of the block, through Stockholm's shouting cyclists and gesticulating citizenry and there before us, just as the Promised Land must have disclosed itself to the harassed tribes of Israel, was a great square and on its further side, the huge sign of the Hotel Stockholm.

After our recent experiences with hotels, we were quite prepared to have the porter tell us there were no rooms. Our luck had changed, however. We not only had rooms, but they were gorgeous rooms—rooms with awning-shaded balconies looking out over the city—rooms with fresh flowers on the tables—rooms with great bathrooms containing bathtubs big enough to swim in and bath towels like blankets. Being good, plumbing-conscious Americans, we were very, very happy.

Later that afternoon, we walked through the beautiful park called Kungsträdgården and suddenly came out on the water front between the Opera House and the Grand Hotel.

To anyone accustomed to the sordid, chopped-up commercialism of our big American cities, the first view of the Stockholm water front is something to be remembered. On our left was the low, broad bridge which carries the traffic from the main part of the city to the islands which block the entrance to Lake Mälar. To the left of the bridge the orange-red awnings of the Grand Hotel glowed in the evening sun. Everywhere were boats; little white steamers waiting to take their daily commuting passengers back to their summer homes; private motorboats, there for the same purpose; sight-seeing boats, fishing boats, all moving about in an atmosphere of quiet orderliness or tied up to the stone quays.

Across the blue water, the Parliament Building and the Royal Palace loomed against the summer sky. We suddenly realized that Stockholm is one of the beautiful cities of the world. We never changed our opinion.

That night we dined at the Grand, where we had been fortunate enough to secure a table beside one of the broad windows that look out over the harbor. It was seven-thirty. Gradually the blue sky faded out and was replaced by aquamarine which shaded off into an iridescent yellow-green along the horizon. Against it the Palace and the Parliament building formed massive black silhouettes.

It was a noble setting for good eating. Within, the modulated chatter of well-fed people, dim lights, and the quiet efficiency of trained waiters. Outside, on the sidewalks and streets just below the window, the constant movement of pedestrians, bicycles, and motor cars. Both inside and out, a carefree atmosphere of gaiety. It was a dream scene in a troubled world—a bit of unreality which shut out, momentarily, the real.

A plane flew across the deepening blue of the sky, its night lights blinking alternately.

16

Stockholm

ON THE SOUTHEAST COAST OF SWEDEN, JUST BELOW THE
bulge, Lake Mälar pours its miles of narrow waters into the Baltic.

Ordinarily lakes have a tendency to avoid oceans and only com-
municate with them through the medium of rivers, but there is
nothing ordinary about Lake Mälar. Instead of keeping modestly
back from the ocean, it has crowded right up to its very shore so
that, if it had not been for the intervention of a group of islands
at its eastern end, it would probably have spilled itself into the
Baltic long before this and disappeared from history forever.

Some seven hundred years ago a Swedish gentleman by the name
of Birger Jarl fortified these islands with the stated intent of
keeping Estonian pirates out of Mälar. It is not clear whether this
was a patriotic or a monopolistic project. That is immaterial, however, for out of this chain of island forts grew Stockholm and for
that Birger Jarl becomes a public benefactor.

Today, the city, which he so inadvertently founded, sits astride
the islands and mushrooms out onto the mainland on either side.
The islands have become steppingstones across the outlet over
which a ceaseless stream of bicycles, trucks, automobiles and blue
trolleys moves restlessly back and forth, while a few feet below, the
waters of Mälar continue to crowd through the narrow channels
between the islands just as they were doing when Birger Jarl first
saw them.

In spite of its ceaseless traffic there is a poise and calm about
Stockholm which makes itself quickly felt. Perhaps it is due to the

126

sparkling blue water which keeps coming into view around every corner—dancing water on which thousands of little boats bob peacefully beside the high stone quays. Perhaps it is due to the quiet, flower-scented parks and squares, their benches filled with sun-worshipers, faces uptilted and eyes closed. Perhaps it is the absence of automobile horns. Perhaps it is the noiseless blue trolleys and the swarms of bicycles which make the traffic appear to glide through the streets. Perhaps it is the monumental buildings scattered so lavishly about the city, which impart a sense of serene age and solidity.

Probably it is due to all these things, but, whatever the cause, one feels unhurried in Stockholm. Because there is so much to see, there is no great urge to see it. Tomorrow will always do, and for today one may sit on a bench at the edge of the quay and watch the rubberneck boats go by or the streams of bicycles passing over the bridge to the middle island or the people strolling in the Kungsträdgården—or just sit.

If it is necessary to introduce sex into the subject, I would say that Stockholm is a female city. It is female in its tidiness, in its sparkle, in the variety of its moods. It is female just as New York is male. The traffic of New York is heavy, ponderous and menacing. It gives out a roar which has only one sex. The traffic in Stockholm, on the other hand, is the antithesis of all this. It is relatively noiseless, it moves faster than that of New York and it has a peculiar quality of lightness.

Stockholm is a city of color, of flags whipping in the breeze, of orange awnings, of unexpected beds of brightly colored flowers, of green parks and red cabs and blue water.

There are undoubtedly many excellent hotels in Stockholm. The trouble is that everyone wants to stay at the Grand. To make life harder for travel agents, the only rooms in the Grand in which

anyone is willing to be found asleep are those along the front looking across the harbor at the Royal Palace.

It is not strange that this should be so, for there are few hotels
in the world where one can lie abed and look out across sun-
flecked water into a king's bedroom. Although no one could tell us
just where the royal chambers were located, the general idea
fascinated us. It apparently fascinates everyone else with the result
that, in order to assure anyone of a front room at the Grand,
reservations should be made for him at birth.

Sydney Clark, incidentally, does not consider sleeping in the
Grand to be worth the effort and casts his vote for the Hotel
Stockholm where we stayed; and, in its very different way, the
Stockholm is quite as extraordinary as the Grand. It is located on
the sixth and seventh floors of a huge office building which covers
a city block and one side of which faces the Norrmalmstorg, a great
square through which the traffic weaves endlessly day and night.

Its awninged balconies look out over the parks and roof tops of
the city. Within, it is a dream of chromium steel efficiency. George
once remarked that it reminded him of a safe-deposit vault. Perhaps so, but it was certainly the most comfortable one in which
we had ever stayed.

Among its many unique characteristics, the Stockholm Hotel
has no restaurant. We breakfasted the first morning in a little shop
nearby called Nybrogård, and located on Nybrogatan. One could
not resist a place with a name and address like that. We had read
about it in Sydney Clark's book. It was a pint-sized job, neat as a
pin, with ivy growing on its inside walls. The Swedes are crazy
for ivy clinging to the walls of their rooms. You are apt to enter
a Swedish living room through a green arch of the stuff. It is
crawling up the sides of the windows and in the morning bath one
looks up, half-expecting to find it twined around the shower head.

On a table in the corner was a great pot of coffee from which we helped ourselves. At a little counter one could buy rolls and a ham-and-lettuce dish. Butter could be had, but you must know the management. A few businessmen with brief cases were hurrying through their breakfast in much the same way that businessmen hurry through their breakfasts in New York and London. Two workmen in overalls ate stolidly, and an unhealthy-looking young man in the corner was joined by an extraordinary blonde in gray slacks whom Lucy hopefully put down as an international spy.

It all seemed very Continental and romantic to George and me and also ridiculously cheap, a factor which always had its charm for us both. But Lucy and Sara were still intent on their hopeless search for an American breakfast. In the days that followed, we roamed restlessly through the neighborhood seeking the orange juice, ham and eggs and buttered toast which were not there.

In spite of its antipathy to food the Stockholm Hotel did serve breakfast in the bedrooms, and in desperation we even tried that. I consider breakfasting in a friend's room before the beds are made to be one of the great tests of friendship. I will even go so far as to admit that it is an equally severe test for a friend to breakfast in mine under similar conditions.

In any event, it failed to solve the problem for Lucy and Sara and it had definite personal disadvantages. We had a corner room from which one could look out over the park, and it was the natural choice for our meeting place. I found it trying, however, to have good-looking Swedish maids coming into my bedroom with trays regardless of whether I was quite ready to receive good-looking maids with trays.

We should not have been disturbed, for we had long since accepted the fact that no Scandinavian maid, valet, or porter ever dreams of knocking on a bedroom door. It is a matter of professional honor with them. Attempt to lock them out, and they will open the door with a passkey in disapproving silence. They have a matchless poise which shrinks from nothing. It was a challenge which I could never meet, however. Years of trouser-wearing had weakened my character, and I found it impossible to clear off tables with any dignity in shirttails.

With the exception of breakfast, however, eating in Stockholm is no problem. In fact the food is so good and so cheap that the only problem is to keep from eating too much of it. We devoured it appreciatively in the vaulted cellars of Den Gyldene Freden, surrounded by the narrow, medieval alleys of Old Stockholm. We sipped our wine at the Grand and at the Operakällaren, watching the twilight deepen over the harbor. We gorged ourselves in the lush aristocracy of the Riche, and at the Trianon we ate exotic food on a tiny island, and watched undersized freight trains moving across the railroad bridge a few feet away.

Dining on the town is a relaxed and informal affair. Anything goes as long as you do not throw things and eventually pay the check. When you dine in someone's home, however, it is well to remember that you are now entering a realm where almost every gastronomic move was crystallized long before you were born.

We had heard so much about the ground rules of Swedish social eating that we approached our first dinner party like a group of rustics in Old England who have been invited to the Manor House for Christmas Eve goings-on.

There should be a rulebook on the subject and rule number one would undoubtedly be: Get there on time. Do not try to show how used you are to this sort of thing by barging in with a shout and halloo half an hour late. That may add to the over-all gaiety of things in the United States, but it is not funny in Sweden.

As you enter the door you are apt to see a leather-covered board on the hall table in which are inserted little cards. These contain the names of the guests and show where they are to sit. Have a good look. You are supposed to take in the girl whose card is to the right of yours and it may be your last chance to identify her, for introductions at these dinners are apt to be on the mumbly side.

In deference to your native land, you may be served a Martini. If it happens to be a good one, bear in mind that this is only a preliminary bout.

You will also be offered some rather oily hors d'oeuvres. Their main purpose it to put you into the best possible physical condition for the work to come. Eat them. The Scandinavians know their onions—or, to be more exact, their pickled herring.

In a few minutes the dining-room doors will be opened. If you are used to standing around for an hour before being fed, you may feel that they are rushing things a bit, but when you look at the table you will realize that when these people decide to be hospitable, they don't do things halfway.

Beside your plate is a formidable row of glasses. In a moment the little round one will be filled with *snaps*. Don't grab it and toss it off, or raise it to your host saying: "Nice to be here, Gus." Watch him, for at this moment he is turning over in his mind the Speech of Welcome.

Americans have the reputation of being born speechmakers, but they are amateurs compared with the Scandinavians, from whom speeches flow as water from a faucet, and who can turn on a five-minute talk at any time of the day or night without ever clawing the air for a word or a phrase. And if you are one of the guests of honor, your host will convey to you the feeling that this is the crowning moment of his life

Having finished his speech, he will then raise his glass and look in turn at each person at the table, bowing almost imperceptibly and murmuring: "*Skål.*" You now raise your glass and murmur, "*Skål,*" also looking at everyone at the table in turn and bowing imperceptibly to each.

Having caught everyone's eye, let it go at that. Don't go on staring meaningfully at them while you drink. Lower your eyes modestly. If you are *skåling* a lovely Swedish woman it will be a great temptation to keep your eyes fixed on her like a wounded deer. Resist it courageously.

Skåling has many of the characteristics of square dancing. Having drunk, you have now reached the second movement. Hold your glass in your hand, look everyone at the table in the eye and bow imperceptibly. That completes the round and you can relax until the next one.

Do not feel, however, that just because the Speech of Welcome and the initial *skåling* are over, that the rest of the evening is on a catch-as-catch-can basis. Scandinavia detests the lone drinker. If you are a male, and thirsty, you can meet the eyes of anyone at the table, raise your glass, and murmur *"Skål"* whenever and as often as you please. If you are unfortunate enough to be a female, however, you are out of luck. You must wait until some male asks you to drink in much the same way that other girls than you, fair reader, have waited in former days for some male to ask them to dance.

Occasionally, thirst gets the better of female reticence and you will find yourself nudged by the lady on your right or left and reminded that she is dry as a camel and to get on your job. It would never occur to her, however, no matter how she might be suffering, to sneak one on the quiet.

Lucy is a lover of good wine, especially after Martinis and *snaps*. She found it hard to remember this restriction on her sex and was apt to reach absent-mindedly for her wine glass. The host was always on the lookout for such gaucheries, however, and before she could get her glass to her lips, his was raised with a resounding *"Skål"* and her honor was saved.

It is important to remember that at a large dinner one must not *skål* the hostess. Every precaution is taken to insure her lasting through the evening.

At the time that the *snaps* is served, the glass to the right will be filled with beer. This does not mean that the party has turned into a beer night. It is merely to help you wash down the *snaps*—just as the wine which follows is, presumably, to wash down the beer.

Now let us suppose that you are sitting on the left of the hostess and that you have passed through the successive stages of *snaps*, beer, white and/or red wine, and a choice of port or sherry with the dessert, without bringing disgrace to your house. The dessert has been passed twice according to custom. It is now your privilege to make the Speech of Thanks.

All that is required of you is that it be light, witty, and graceful. Pat and Mike stories, and tales of farmers' daughters do not qualify. Its purpose is to thank the host and hostess both personally and on behalf of the other guests for their hospitality. At this point in the evening you should have no difficulty with this pleasant formality.

After dinner you will have brandy and then, if your host is doing well financially, there may be highballs. If you are the guest of honor remember, if possible, that no one can go until you do, but, on the other hand, do not forget that it is not polite for the guest of honor to leave too early.

Should you be traveling in your own car, as we were, do not travel in it on the nights you dine out. Take a taxi. The Swedish police are very old-fashioned about these things, and if by this time your blood content does not contain more than the legally allowed .002 (*two pro mille*) of alcohol you probably need a transfusion.

If you really want to feel Swedish, bow over the hostess' hand as you are leaving and murmur: "*Tack för maten.*" Never mind what it means. Just say it. You are in the act of leaving anyway, so the risk is very slight.

Just two other points and the Scandinavian dinner is over. On the following day it will do no harm if you send flowers and write a little note. Also, the next time you see your host or hostess, do not forget to thank them, and profusely, for their kindness—if you want to be asked again.

17

More Stockholm—
and a Bit of Visby

SCATTERED LIKE STARDUST OVER THE WATERS TO THE east of Stockholm are thousands of small islands known as the Skärgården.

A hospitable Swedish friend, who had a summer home on one of them, asked us to spend the day with him. He met us in a motorboat a few miles south of Stockholm, and we wound among the rocky, fir-covered little islands for such a long time that we wondered how anyone could ever hope to find their way back through the maze.

Our hostess had prepared a picnic lunch which was laid out on a red-and-white tablecloth, spread on the smooth surface of a great rock. A few feet below us the waters of the Baltic slapped gently against the granite sides of our island. The sun warmed the rough surface of the rock. A small lizard crawled out of a crevice, looked us over and went back into his hiding place to sit it out until we had gone.

When Lucy and I give a picnic lunch on the shores of Martha's Vineyard, everyone gets a couple of sandwiches, a hard-boiled egg, if they are quick enough, and a bit of fruit. Each time that we were exposed to Scandinavian hospitality, however, we were shamed by such memories, for when these generous people open their doors they open them wide and there appears to be nothing too good for the incoming guest and no effort too great if it adds to his comfort and pleasure.

This particular lunch, for example, started with *snaps* and beer, pickled herring, onion and thin slices of bread and butter. There followed ham, meat loaf, the inevitable boiled potatoes, tomatoes eaten like apples, several kinds of cheese and, finally, fruit and coffee.

That evening, our host had promised to introduce us to the crayfish.

To anyone unfamiliar with Swedish customs and folkways, let me say that the crayfish is to Sweden what Coca-Cola, the hamburger, hot dogs, apple pie and doughnuts are, in the aggregate, to the United States.

But even that is an inadequate statement. For there is a relationship between the crayfish and the Swedes which goes much deeper. It is intangible—one might almost call it mystical. A Swede speaks of Crayfish as a Frenchman speaks of Love, or a Yale man of the Skull and Bones. One feels occasionally as if one were standing on thresholds beyond which dim paths lead back to Maypoles and druidic rites.

All of which adds up to the fact that the Swedes go wild about crayfish. I approach the subject with diffidence and would gladly side-step it entirely, but to do so would be like writing of the Old West without mentioning the Indians.

The crayfish is really not a fish at all, but is built more on the model of a miniature lobster from four to six inches long. Their tails, in the cooked state at least, are curled forward and pressed tightly against their stomachs and their eyes are big, black, and protruding—eyes which seem to follow you, even in death, wherever you move.

Our charming hostess set a huge bowl of the creatures on the dining-room table and our host gave us detailed instructions on how to manipulate them.

First we were given a special knife to be placed where the

animal's neck would have been if it had a neck, and to be used for decapitation. Personally, I dislike decapitating animals alive or dead, but when they watch me during the process with beady, accusing eyes it makes me feel like one of the Borgias whose heart was not in his work.

Our host then showed us how to break off the tail and set it aside for future use. He then taught us to remove the red armor plate from the back of the mangled body.

"Now," he said, and there was a look of ecstasy on his face, "you take the underside of the body—so—press it to the lips—so—and suck."

If you have a cold crab around the house, press its stomach to your mouth and you will get the idea. I kissed my first crayfish without passion and set it on the plate as the basis for the pile that I knew I was expected to create.

Then came the tail. That was the *pièce de résistance*; the heart of the artichoke. Nature has protected the underside of the crayfish's tail with a series of steel-like bands designed to shield it from prying vandals such as I. It is the custom to break these bands with the thumbs, which is only comparable to using the thumbs for breaking up barbed-wire entanglements. Mine became so sore that I lost most of the meat in the struggle. After many failures, I brought forth one tail assembly intact. Everyone applauded. I reached for the *snaps*.

Later that night we got into our host's motorboat for the return trip to the mainland. On an island to the east there suddenly rose through the blackness a barrage of skyrockets, and the distant shore was lined with red fire.

It was the direction from which Uncle Joe would have come if he had decided to go visiting. "What is that?" I asked, somewhat anxiously.

"That," he said, "is to celebrate the opening of the crayfish season."

It was one o'clock before we got back to the Hotel Stockholm that night, and at five-thirty we rose again to take the morning plane to Visby. It was not a genial group which set out for the flying field without benefit of breakfast, and it would have taken little persuasion to deprive Visby of our visit.

The island of Gotland lies off the southeast coast of Sweden, about an hour by plane from Stockholm, and Visby is its capital. It is not an upstart town like Stockholm, but has been weathering on this same spot for thirteen hundred years. A thousand years ago it was the trade center of northern Europe, which is just three hundred years before Birger Jarl thought of doing anything about keeping the Estonian pirates out of Lake Mälar.

According to modern standards, it is incredible that such a small town should have occupied such an important place in history. Its principal interest today lies in the two miles of battlemented walls which enclose its medieval buildings and ancient churches just as they did a thousand years ago. They are crumbling here and there, but that is the right of any wall after a thousand years.

Approaching Visby from the air involves a certain amount of dramatic shock, for at a height of a few hundred feet the ravages of time are not so obvious, and one might have been snatched back through the centuries to days when the twisting streets below were bustling with men in fur-trimmed cloaks and page boys preceded women wearing tall, conical hats.

In spite of the antiquarian feast which so obviously awaited us, my instinct told me that after four and a half hours' sleep, some of the banquet guests might not have much appetite. In fact, Sara and Lucy had stated their opinion of the expedition quite clearly before we boarded the plane. Now they looked down on the ancient battlements with unromantic eyes.

"Why it's just a little bit of a thing," said Sara, scornfully; "when does the plane go back?"

"Five o'clock," I said uncomfortably.

"Five!" cried Sara, indignantly. "Why we can see this in half an hour."

"I've seen it now," said Lucy, who was always one to gang up and particularly dangerous when tired.

Our first move on entering the town was to engage two double bedrooms at the hotel. With these in reserve, George and I felt safer.

After breakfast, even Lucy and Sara had a temporary return of vitality. We went to the Gotland Tourist Association which occupies the ground floor of a medieval, half-timbered building and there acquired the services of a guide and an automobile. Our guide was a young man of obvious intelligence, but his heart was in the present rather than the past. He was a Visby boy, sick of old ruins and desiring nothing more than to see his home town grow and take a bigger and more realistic place in the world about it.

We did not know that, however, and were somewhat surprised when he took us first to the botanical gardens. Quite obviously this was an enterprise which he considered worthy of special attention. He forced us to drag our exhausted bodies along the flower-bordered paths while he told us the names of the rare trees and plants along the way.

We eventually left the gardens and after a hasty glance at the old buildings inside the walls, he told the driver to take us to the new section which lies outside; and there, where once the round, striped tents of besieging enemies dotted the hillsides, he showed us the new workers' apartments and the primary and secondary schools which he considered fine examples of what can be done with an active Chamber of Commerce.

We learned during the course of his discussions that he was planning to have us lunch at a large resort hotel about ten miles outside the city and that in the afternoon he intended to take us for a long drive around the island—undoubtedly to inspect some modernistic factories.

Our breakfast calories had long since burned out. Lucy and Sara went into open rebellion. They knew about that bedroom at the hotel and they were not going to waste it. They agreed to go as far as the seaside resort and there to dismiss both the guide and the car. We would then have a simple lunch—did we understand what they meant—a *simple* lunch—something based on tea and toast. After that they proposed to take a taxi back to Visby and go to bed—quick.

When our driver heard of this change in plan, be became temporarily deranged. He pressed the accelerator down to the floor. The venerable car began to emit loose, roaring sounds and shot forward through the narrow streets, grazing the corners of ancient buildings and making frantic lunges at passing bicycles. We explained to our guide that we were very early and in no hurry whatsoever. He merely shrugged his shoulders silently.

At the big hotel, we found that table reservations had been made for us by the Tourist Association and that, for some reason, the hotel had become convinced we were VIP's. An American flag stood in the center of our table. The headwaiter rushed to welcome us and to take our order for what he assured us was to be a very special luncheon—none of the trash which the other guests were eating.

Lucy and Sara said that all they wanted was an omelet, a pot of tea, and, *please*, some water. They also indicated that if this could be done quickly it would be okay with them. Obviously their primary thought was to get lunch over with and slip into that hotel bedroom.

The headwaiter was chagrined. No wine? No *spécialité de la maison?* He glanced at the little American flag, apparently debating whether or not to remove it. Then the philosophic discipline which controls all headwaiters regained the ascendancy. He allowed an ordinary waiter to take our extraordinary order and disappeared—forever.

In an effort to achieve simplicity, according to American standards, Lucy and Sara succeeded in achieving chaos. One half-hour later, a pot of tea was produced. At this point the American flag was definitely removed. The management had come to the conclusion that it should not wave above a pot of tea.

Thirty minutes later when the tea had long since been consumed, a small omelet appeared and later, after repeated threats of a vague nature on the part of George, the waiter brought a split of charged water.

He was evidently much puzzled as to just what kind of a meal we were trying to have. We were beginning to share his bewilderment.

Eventually we dropped Lucy and Sara at the hotel, after which George and I loaded ourselves with cameras and set out to shoot the sights on foot. We staggered, exhausted, through the narrow, winding streets, bordered by twisted one-storied houses as old as the battlemented walls which overshadowed them. We peered through gates at trim little postage-stamp gardens, their gravel walks bordered with thin slabs of sandstone. Sailors of the Swedish navy stood about in picturesque groups, silhouetted against the gray ruins of churches, and looked bored. Artists painted rather badly at street corners. Rattling buses thundered past at breakneck speed.

We snapped pictures with the abandon of men too weary to

reckon cost and flew back to Stockholm through the twilight to eat a sleepy supper at the Grand while a great white yawl maneuvered itself up to the edge of the quay a few feet from our table.

We really did not see much of Stockholm from a guidebook point of view. After a month of traveling, we were beginning to show signs of wear at the corners. Gone the days when we could canter along steadily from nine in the morning until midnight without collapsing somewhere along the way. Senility was beginning to raise its palsied head. Our hotel rooms assumed an increasing importance in our lives, and we began to look forward to that delightful period in the late afternoon when we could totter to our beds, slip off our shoes and collapse for an hour before dinner.

Sara and Lucy, who had started out as two of the most eager of beavers, had undergone a change comparable to that of Dr. Jekyll in his transition to Mr. Hyde. Their attitude toward points of interest had passed through all stages from Must to Must Not. Their one desire now was to sit in the sun like the good burghers of Stockholm and never again to behold a castle, a church, or a museum.

This was, of course, a highly unintellectual attitude and one which irritated George and me who, as practical men, believed in getting *something* for our money. And so it came to pass that our sight-seeing life was best symbolized by the Volga Boatmen, straining against the ropes as they pull their heavily laden craft slowly up the river.

It is significant, however, that each day the Boatmen made some progress and each day, spurred on by that rigid disciplinarian, Sydney Cark, we saw a few things that we should have seen although we also left undone many things that we ought to have done.

We drove, for example, to Skansen, Sweden's biggest outdoor

museum, to which the Swedes have dragged old buildings from the frozen tundras of Lapland and the golden wheatfields of Skåne. It was an enormous place. George and I did not let Lucy and Sara see the official map that was handed to us at the entrance gate, but at the end of two hours they unfortunately stumbled on one tacked to a bulletin board and discovered that they were only halfway around. They immediately crawled back to the car and collapsed indignantly.

We dragged them to the Town Hall, protesting every foot of the way. Here for a brief moment, their flagging vitality revived, however, for the most extraordinary thing about Stockholm's Town Hall is that its reality outstrips its publicity. This is praise indeed, as it is the most touted building in Scandinavia. Every once in a while man creates something which in its field approaches perfection. It is such a rare quality that it is immediately recognizable even by the uninitiated. We received few complaints about the Town Hall once we had reached it. Sara and Lucy merely returned to their rooms and passed out quietly. It was a high tribute to a beautiful building.

We saw many other places, but it was far from an adequate coverage. But perhaps it was the best way to see a city. We saw it mostly through leisurely lunches and dinners with charming people. We saw it as we walked about its streets and sat in its parks. We saw it as we leaned over the railings of the hotel balcony, as we browsed in its stores and wandered through its streets. We saw it casually and that turned out to be a good way.

The memories that one brings away from any place are made up of many small things, as a wall is made up of many stones.

Stockholm to us was brilliant color and sparkling water, blue trolleys in tandem, tree-shaded parks, the big NK sign revolving against the sky on its lacy steel base, the difficulty of remembering to walk on the left-hand side and the irritation caused by stubborn

Swedes who bump into people that persist in drifting over to the right, Gustavus Adolphus Square at noon, with the workers sitting on every available projection, soaking up the sun, the sound of street conversations which, filtered through American ears, cause a male Swede passing the time of day to sound angry, while a female similarly engaged might be singing love songs.

Stockholm is stone quays, rubberneck boats dashing out from under bridges, Drottingham Palace and Theater, the unaccountable lack of blondes, the red-white-and-blue awnings of the department store across the street from our hotel, where the flags of England, France and the United States whipped in the fresh breeze, Prince Eugen's home at Valdemarsudde, the blue waters of the Saltsjön, bridges and bicycles—always bicycles.

Near the hotel is a little park named Berzelii. Past its deeply shaded lawns and flower beds the traffic of the city flows unheeded. Preoccupied businessmen with brief cases occasionally hurry along its paved walks, but its real life revolves around an open-sided marquee under which there is a food stand. Scattered about nearby are little metal tables, each shaded by a red and green umbrella and rows of benches for those who are content to sit and watch others eat.

I stopped on my way back to the hotel and found a seat on one of the benches. A few feet away two men were drinking beer and talking earnestly together. At the next table a girl carried on a listless conversation with two male companions over a pot of coffee. A gray-haired man read his paper and sipped a glass of milk. A man and a woman were drinking what looked like raspberry sodas. Pigeons strutted.

A rough-looking man clutched his empty glass and stared moodily at the pigeons. At the next table a character in a black Homburg and a savage expression watched his wife demolish a high dish of ice cream. A young man in a purple shirt, black tie, and soiled white shorts strolled past, his arms folded. People queued up at the food stand.

Under the trees in the distance, the sun glinted on the shiny sides of the blue trolleys, and the legs of the cyclists moved rhythmically up and down.

18

South Sweden

IT IS HARD TO LEAVE STOCKHOLM. THERE IS A SIREN-LIKE quality about the place which keeps the wanderer hanging around like Ulysses, long after his conscience tells him that he should be on his way.

To make up for the sadness of parting, however, Sweden had put on its best bib and tucker. As we rolled toward the southwest over a broad two-lane parkway, the fleecy clouds which had come to symbolize this country for us as much as its blue-and-yellow flag, staged a special parade using only their plumpest representatives. On either side the rolling fields were dotted with hay cones, or covered with golden blankets of wheat through which the ripples ran like waves before the fresh breeze to break against dark-green clumps of trees on the horizon.

This was the road which connected Stockholm with the big industrial cities—the "Köpings"—Nyköping, Norrköping, Linköping, Jönköping—it was the road which led to Swedish glass, Swedish ball bearings, Swedish matches, Swedish steel, and all those other products on which the world has stamped the name "Swedish" as a warranty of quality and precision.

It was one of the great industrial arteries of Europe, but in spite of this it had no connection with dirt or dinginess, with smoke-belching chimneys, shoddy housing or screaming billboards. To those trained to regard such eyesores as an essential part of national production it was a bit bewildering; but Sweden does not seem to know the meaning of such things.

While we were discussing this phenomenon, Lucy developed a violent head cold.

We lunched that day in pine woods, devoid as usual of underbrush and carpeted with moss—and as usual our lunch consisted of fresh bread, cheese, and marmalade. But on this day a new ingredient was added—bees. They surrounded us in friendly groups. They sat on our food and watched the approach of our champing jaws with fearless eyes. When we moved away, they came with us. We were entering the Swedish bee belt, but no one realized it yet except the bees.

We also had our first experience with gasoline at seventy-five cents a gallon. It was a shock to part with ten dollars for a tankful of gas, an emotional crisis similar to that induced by the check for a few rounds of drinks at a New York night club. It helped somewhat that the station attendant was frequently a good-looking Swedish girl, but the relief was only temporary. It made us feel grateful to Scandinavia for being so small and it explained why the roads are so free of private automobiles—and so full of bicycles.

Gränna is a lovely old village, slumbering on the eastern shore of Lake Vättern. About two miles to the south, on a high ridge overlooking the lake, stands the Gyllene Uttern (or Golden Otter, if you prefer), a favorite stopping-off point on the road connecting south Sweden with Stockholm.

The architecture of the Otter is as extraordinary as its name, ranging from a peasant sod hut to a medieval castle. One gets the impression that there must have been a landslide at some time in the past which pushed all the houses in the neighborhood into a pile and mixed them up rather thoroughly in the process. In the great graveled area before the entrance a restless stream of undersized English and Swedish cars, stuffed like sausages with baggage and passengers, was constantly arriving and departing.

147

Lucy glanced at the Otter with swollen, uninterested eyes, seized her box of paper handkerchiefs and retired to her bed with a bottle of aureomycin and a temperature. It was our first real casualty and a miserable bit of timing, for we had a room at the Otter which called for appreciation. It was a huge chamber with a private balcony from which one could look over the blue lake and down onto a stone, flag-bordered terrace where the tourists from the buses and cars kept moving out to look at the lake and up at the balcony. It made us feel like the Royal Family showing themselves to their people.

The discovery that the room was swarming with bees was disconcerting. Perhaps the word "swarming" is an exaggeration. The majority were sitting quietly on the windowpanes attending to their business, but it so happens that neither of us trust bees. You can never tell what they may consider their business to be.

I chased them out with some diffidence and shut all doors and windows. They immediately came crawling back under the French doors leading to the balcony. Apparently they had been through this experience before and knew just what to do. We gave up and lived in a kind of combination apiary-bedroom for the next few days. I will say in behalf of Swedish bees, however, that at no time during the period did they show anything but courteous indifference.

Immediately after breakfast on the following morning George collapsed with the same disease. We divided our dwindling stock of aureomycin, and with very real regret I wired the Park Avenue Hotel at Göteborg canceling our reservations.

It was raining and altogether a good day for being sick. Sara and I explored the little one-street village, seeking local color for ourselves and paper handkerchiefs for George and Lucy. Gränna was not an easy shopping town, however, as most of its stores seemed devoted to the sale of an odd confection called Polkagrisar. This is a kind of candy stick striped like a barber's pole for which Gränna appears to have a world reputation.

It's an odd thing about reputations, as Sara very properly remarked during the course of our vain, damp search for paper handkerchiefs. For centuries a village takes its part in the stream of history. It is blessed with a beautiful location. It produces statesmen, scholars, historians, explorers, and artists out of all proportion to its size. Battles are fought on its heights which have changed Sweden's future. To the current world, however, it is known for one thing—Polkagrisar.

We drove down the slope to the edge of the lake where the flower farms are located. There we passed through acres and acres of unbelievable blooms—and for the first time we understood about the bees.

On the ridge between the hotel and the village is a lovely bronze monument depicting two somewhat immodest, but decidedly well knit young Swedes finishing a foot race. There is no good reason why it should be in this particular spot; it is typical of the Scandinavian people that they should have gone to the trouble and expense of putting it there merely because it is beautiful.

The straining figures are wonderfully realistic. Every muscle and sinew stands out under the bronze skin. The rain had stopped a half-hour before and glistening drops still clung to the bodies of the runners. Sara gazed at them fascinated. "Never have I seen such detail," she exclaimed, "even beads of sweat!" She suddenly clapped her hands to her head. "My God, it's running off them!"

Two days later, the aureomycin had done its amazing work and we were on our way south to Skåne, the great breadbasket of Sweden which lies at its southern tip.

Here everything was big. The farms, the red buildings, the yellow fields, all had lost the toylike look of the north country. It was a land of blue lakes and forests, and rippling wheat—a land of broad roads down which huge logging trucks thundered and bounced.

We ate our picnic lunch in a pine forest under trees which rose like masts from a floor of fine grass and moss. Alternate bars of shadow and sunlight slanted down through the branches. It seemed a desecration to eat bread and marmalade in such a cathedral setting.

Late that afternoon we came out on the west coast at Halmstad and motored south beside the blue waters of the Kattegat to the little seaside resort of Båstad. Across the Kattegat was Denmark. On our left extending to the horizon were golden carpets of wheat, flecked with red barns whose roofs were mossed to the north.

As usual, the last half-hour before arriving at a new place was a period of tension and strain for George and me. Lucy and Sara had become firmly convinced that Båstad was a seaside dump and they predicted gloatingly a boardwalk lined with salt-water-taffy stands, shooting galleries and ring-toss games.

The discovery, therefore, that the Hotel Skånegården was, if anything, more beautiful than Sydney Clark had described it, was a relief at least to George and me, although perhaps momentarily disappointing to Sara and Lucy. It was a low, brick structure built around a series of gardens and approached from the street through an arched gateway. Once inside, we were surrounded by flowers and color—and bees.

We walked down to the shore before dinner, past the tennis courts where the late King Gustaf V played so often. Near the beach George discovered a large building which housed a restaurant on the ground floor and advertised an exposition of paintings on the floor above. Being always one to develop the cultural side of life he decided immediately that it was his duty to investigate.

On the terrace he found a woman of unquestioned physical merit, but with something less than complete understanding of the English language. The following extraordinary conversation followed:

"What is the exposition on the second floor?"

"They are paintings."

"Are they good paintings?"

"Nay, nay."

"I mean, are they by the best Swedish artists?"

"Magazines."

"You mean illustrations?"

"Nay, English."

"English artists?"

"Nay."

"Tack. We'll be back tomorrow."

"Nay, nay."

Lucy and Sara and George disappeared to their luxurious rooms for predinner shut-eye. Feeling that someone should stay awake in the face of so much beauty, I climbed a hill behind the village. Far below lay the great arc of the shore line, while to the west the tawny wheat carpets of Skåne extended to the horizon dotted with farm buildings and villages. The red-tiled roofs of Båstad contrasted sharply against the blue waters of the bay, and immediately below was a little flower-bordered park with two great trees on either side of a pool. Casual voices rose from the village. A cuckoo sounded somewhere in the woods, further up the hill.

I walked back to the hotel through little side streets paved with cobblestones laid in semicircles. On every side were flowers. The air was heavy with their scent and in the gardens people were eating supper or drinking beer, apparently contented with their lot—as well they might be.

The following morning was Sunday. We had planned to breakfast in the main garden. When we arrived, there were many people doing the same thing. In the clear morning air it was much too beautiful to be real. We sat down at a vacant table and were immediately covered with bees.

Everyone else was similarly covered, but no one appeared to mind in the least. The various groups went on talking and laughing gaily through gray mists of bees. We were old-fashioned about such things, however, and retreated to one of the cloistered porches. Here the bees gave us up except for an occasional individualist which perished in the marmalade.

People had told us all sorts of stories about Swedish bathing customs. Immediately after breakfast, therefore, we made a dash for the beach in order to get a favorable position and miss nothing of an educational nature.

It is hard to tell just what the hinterlands of our immature minds were expecting. What we saw were some pleasant-looking Swedish women in one-piece bathing suits, some well-built Swedish men in skimpy trunks and swarms of young Swedish fry in the starko. We had evidently been misled or come to the wrong beach.

There were bathhouses, but everyone seemed to prefer dressing at home, a situation which provided the only notable incident in connection with the Båstad beachhead.

The Swedish women of Båstad appeared to have a universal aversion to wet bathing suits. As each female bather emerged from the water, she put on a bathrobe and faced a high wooden jetty. With a few deft movements, she somehow or other slipped out of the bathing suit without disturbing the bathrobe or the onlookers. These daughters of Houdini then calmly tied the sashes of their bathrobes, placed their bathing suits in little bags, gave the field a thought-you-were-going-to-see-something-didn't-you kind of a look, and started nonchalantly for home.

The men's bathing suits were so inconsequential that they did not have to worry about the harmful effect of wet material. They just went home.

On the following morning we left Båstad for Hälsingborg, where we were to leave Sweden and take the ferry for Denmark.

The ferry slip gleamed with white paint as did the ferryboat bobbing in its wooden arms. I dashed into the Swedish custom-house which stood next to it, to find out what was required of us.

At home, it might have taken an hour to attract anyone's attention. A young man, who spoke impeccable English, came forward immediately. He said that nothing was required until we boarded the ferry, at which time a cursory inspection of our baggage might take place. If we hurried, he said, we would please catch the ferry that was just leaving. He came from behind the counter, accompanied me to the door and bowed deeply.

On the ferry we were met by the Danish customs officials. "Welcome to Denmark," they said, somewhat prematurely, but none the less cordially. No, there would be no inspection, cursory or otherwise. The trip would take twenty minutes and they wanted us to enjoy each and every one of them. They hoped that our stay in Denmark would be a memorable one.

It was.

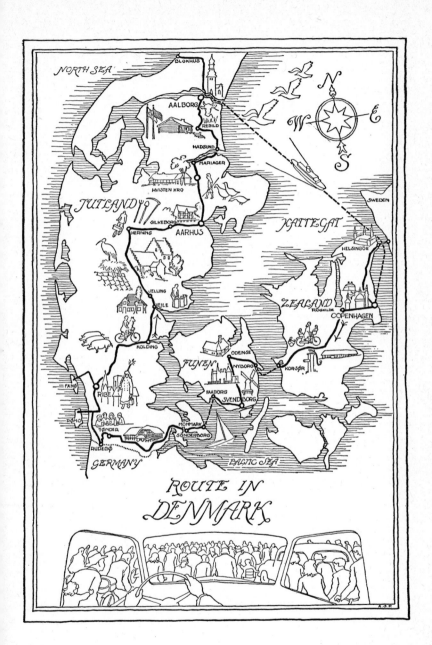

ROUTE IN DENMARK

Denmark

19

Copenhagen

THE ODD YEARNING FOR SIMILITUDE WHICH SEEMS TO BE one of Man's incurable mental diseases has caused Copenhagen to be referred to as the Paris of the North. But that is just making things unnecessarily complicated, for Copenhagen is Copenhagen and nothing else—which should be enough for anyone. It is a city old in body but young in spirit. Its carefully preserved rococo buildings carry the ivory patina of ancient photographs, but its twisting, bewildering streets teem with a vitality that is definitely oriented to the future.

Because of this Janus-like quality Copenhagen offers its visitors a richness of fare that involves acute frustration, peptic ulcers and flat feet for those who lack the ability to be selective. It is an incredible banquet of museums, water fronts, churches, night spots, castles, famous restaurants, public buildings, winding streets, twisted towers, parks, shopwindows and—of course—bicycles.

One must choose with discretion or be prepared to take the consequences. And if you are the toxic type who cannot explore historic sites for more than four hours at a time without getting museum feet and staircase knees, or if you are apt to be seized with an uncontrollable desire to sleep after a huge meal—well, the problem will be even more difficult.

For a visitor, the center of any city is the hotel at which he happens to be staying—or perhaps in Scandinavia it is more correct to say, at which he is *lucky* enough to be staying.

In our case it was the d'Angleterre. There are, of course, a number of excellent hotels in Copenhagen, but, just as everyone coming to Stockholm wants to get into the Grand, so do the pilgrims to Copenhagen bow their heads toward the d'Angleterre.

One cannot blame them, for this great, rambling, old-fashioned structure carries within its walls the essential flavor of the city. There is a lushness about it and a prodigal waste of space which belongs to an era when buildings were not planned with any regard for cost per cubic foot and owners conveyed their desires to their architects by waving their arms vaguely toward the horizon.

Occupying an entire block front, the d'Angleterre faces Kongens Nytorv—a great square with a park in the center, around which the traffic swirls madly day and night, pouring in and draining off through a dozen radiating streets. In the center of the park, like a mounted policeman, is a huge equestrian statute of Christian V, irreverently known to the local residents as "The Horse."

A sidewalk café extends across the front of the d'Angleterre, flanking the entrance. Its little tables are occupied from early morning until evening by that mysterious group of cosmopolites who spend a large part of their lives sitting in sidewalk cafés staring glassily at the passing traffic, apparently indifferent as to whether it is made up of camel trains, Rolls Royces or bicycles.

This particular café offers to its patrons, as a special attraction, a unique opportunity to observe and criticize the general appearance and accouterments of all arriving and departing guests of the hotel.

Ordinarily, this would not mean too much, however, as most of the guests who pass in and out of the d'Angleterre look like illustrations in travel folders, and all of them appear to have bought their luggage only a few days previously from the smartest and most expensive shops.

It was only when parties like ours arrived that things livened up a bit. We drew up before the door about two-thirty in the afternoon when a majority of the café customers had finished lunch and were settling down to a quiet hour of staring.

Our luggage had not been purchased recently and was nothing to have stood beside with pride even on the day it was bought. For five weeks we had been adding to it odd paper packages, loose items of clothing and all the battered flotsam-and-jetsam that gathers in the back end of an automobile on a long trip.

Our traveling clothes were also beginning to lose some of their snap. George's and mine had not given out much of a crackle even in their prime. Sara and Lucy had one look at the rows of waxen faces and refused to get out. I went to find porters.

A canary-yellow sports roadster drew up behind us. It was so low that the sleek, begoggled couple in the bucket seats could have dragged their knuckles on the ground. Porters swarmed out and over it, unbuttoning the taut canvas which covered the back seat and removing a mountain of gleaming leather cases. These they tucked beneath their arms and disappeared. There were no more porters. The eyes of the café returned to us.

I let down the tailboard of the Plymouth and began to drag out the battered suitcases, packages, cloth knapsacks, and odd bits of clothing. They lay in a pile on the sidewalk like the sordid belongings of a dispossessed family. A porter came out, looked at the mass distastefully and went back. Lucy and Sara, almost in tears, ran the gantlet of the tables and disappeared into the hotel.

At that moment George saw a combination of lights and shadows in the park across the street which appealed to him as photogenic. He pulled his camera out of the jumble and plunged into the traffic. I was left to face my audience alone.

Our bedroom at the d'Angleterre must have been almost thirty by thirty. It had a vestibule with huge closets leading from it, and in case our possessions refused to be contained in such miserable spaces, great wardrobes were provided for the overflow. There were extra-length sofas for reclining, overstuffed armchairs for lounging, a big desk for writing, oversized beds for sleeping. Everything about the d'Angleterre was on the grand scale.

The bathroom would have been considered a good-sized bedroom in most hotels. Young hippopotami could have wallowed in its tub. To add a touch of mystery, the chain of the toilet disappeared through a hole in the ceiling, never to be seen again, and over the bathtub was another chain which disappeared stealthily in a similar manner and which we never dared to pull.

In spite of its size and its general lavishness, the d'Angleterre was apparently served by a single elevator. It was not even a fast elevator. Yet no congestion or delay ever seemed to result from this fact. The guests at the d'Angleterre stayed put much better than their American counterparts.

The elevator, on our bedroom floor, had a ponderous wooden door which opened outwards and folded back against the wall. Being used to sliding doors, as well as to the necessity of leaping into elevators the instant they came to a stop, we followed our usual practice of ringing the bell and then standing with our noses pressed against the door like apartment-house poodles.

As a result, when the door opened it invariably sent us staggering backward and we would eventually find ourselves pinned behind it. As the elevator was always filled with Continental-looking ladies and gentlemen and their elegant hand luggage, it was difficult to free ourselves immediately and after that it would have looked silly to come popping out as if we had been playing a children's game.

Once the car was empty the elevator operator would promptly swing the door shut and disappear, leaving us flattened against the wall. Fortunately, the sophisticates who had emerged were always so occupied in jabbering animatedly to one another in foreign languages that they never looked back, so we were able to ring again without too much loss of face.

Just inside the entrance to the hotel was the porter's desk, manned by a terrifying personage with two assistants. This was the very Jehovah of all porters—the ultimate in the Order of the Crossed Keys. All day long he faced an impatient group to whom he handed out keys, delivered messages and packages and from whom he received keys, messages, packages, and highly complicated instructions in a dozen languages. All of this he accomplished with a completely dead pan and during it all he licked postage stamps and placed them accurately on postcards. To the casual eye, his department was a scene of chaos, but basically it was a world of stern discipline and ruthless efficiency.

On the sidewalk in front of the hotel reigned another individual —tall, broad-shouldered and handsome, who wore his doorman's coat like an officer of the Guards. His visored cap was set on his head at just the right angle and seemed to say that here was no hotel servant, but some young madcap aristocrat who was playing the part for the afternoon. Lucy and Sara became quite silly on the subject. George and I tried to bolster our dignity by looking haughty and handing the fellow a constant succession of five-kroner notes, but in spite of all our efforts we always felt like schoolboys in his presence.

Behind the sidewalk café large French doors led into the dining room. These were left open on pleasant summer days and one could breakfast there, looking out over the heads of the early café clientele and across the narrow sidewalk at the never-ending flow of silent street traffic.

At the southeast corner of the hotel, a portion of the traffic stream turns right into Strøget which, translated, means "The Stretch." Incidentally this is one of the extraordinary thoroughfares of the world. It connects the square, Kongens Nytorv, with another great square at the western end of the city, the Raadhuspladsen. Strøget is bordered by most of the famous stores of Copenhagen. In width it ranges from an alley-like affair to a broad street and once or twice develops weak places in its sides and blows out into squares where the traffic whirls in all directions and the life of the visiting motorist is a nightmare.

As a climax to its eccentricities, Strøget is only a nickname. The real name of this unpredictable thoroughfare changes every few blocks from Østergade to Amagertorv to Vimmelskaftet to Nygade and finally, to Frederiksberggade. It is rather confusing to anyone taking a walk along its brief length for the first time.

On the morning of our first full day in Copenhagen we ate our eggs and sipped our coffee before one of the French doors watching the morning in-trek of bicycles which converged at the intersection of Gothersgade and Store Kongensgade and flowed past the hotel. They rode easily and tirelessly, these Danes, with a casualness at which we never ceased to wonder. Sitting very straight, they moved forward with the silent relentlessness of Fate itself, occasionally weaving in and out, almost touching, but never quite.

It was a cross section of the world on wheels; pretty stenographers, smartly dressed and paying little heed to the wind which whipped their skirts above their knees; clerks in black Homburgs with brief cases hooked over their straight handle bars; a workman with a ladder casually balanced on his shoulder; grocery and bakers' boys on tricycles making their early morning deliveries; men riding with one hand while with the other they steadied bundles on the narrow baggage racks over their rear wheels; young mothers with infants strapped into handle-bar seats—happy infants apparently fascinated by this suicidal method of transportation.

Two dowagers, dressed to the nines from hairdo to open-toed shoes, pedaled serenely through the melee, chatting animatedly. We could almost hear them saying: "My dear, I stood it as long as I could and then I turned to her and said . . ."

A cripple without feet went by on a tricycle which he propelled with his hands.

Taxicabs and trucks ripped through this human stream. We held our food suspended in horror, waiting for the crash that never came and we understood the meaning of a Danish friend who said: "Did you ever try to hit a Dane on a bicycle? Every time you think you have him, he escapes."

Across the street the park formed a vivid green background for the ever-shifting scene. Over by the Royal Theater the yellow trolleys were squirming restlessly. Above the trees Charlottenborg raised its dull, dim bulk. A sparrow hopped over the sill and began picking crumbs out of the carpet. A second followed and a third. There was a glint of sunlight on "The Horse" in the middle of the park.

We could have sat indefinitely in the frame of the broad doorway, but we had to face the usual problem of getting off dead center on the first morning in any city. It was a problem the answer to which we never seemed to learn. For several day before arriving at an important stopping place each one would read up on the subject in Sydney Clark and Clara Laughlin, or in the mass of travel booklets which were forever scattered over the seats of the car. Each made confidential notes of the things that must be seen.

The difficulty was that each set of notes differed according to the temperament of the maker. Lucy and Sara had, of course, underlined all references to stores. I was what might be known as a General Coverage man. For my money it seemed rather footless to travel halfway around the world in order to visit a city and not pay at least fleeting homage to its principal points of interest. George, on the other hand, would have been quite content to wander planlessly through the streets and parks and along the water fronts, letting the place sink into him through his pores.

We all knew these little idiosyncrasies and the result was that on these first mornings no one wanted to make a suggestion, realizing that it was sure to start an argument. The tension would mount steadily during breakfast, exploding eventually into a heated debate, Lucy declaring that she wasn't going to be dragged through another museum, Sara stating that she wasn't going to spend the day slogging around the hot streets after George who didn't know where he was going anyway, and George and I declaring that we hadn't come to Scandinavia to be trampled to death at bargain counters.

In the end everything was resolved happily by each going his own way. A few hours alone in a big city is like loosening the cork of a champagne bottle. It takes the pressure off.

At first George and I had been worried by these shopping safaris of Lucy and Sara, fearing that they would not leave us enough money to finish the trip. Gradually we discovered, however, that neither of them could ever make up their minds about anything they wanted to buy until the day after we had left the place where it was on sale. Then they knew without a doubt the mistake they had made, which seemed to give them a melancholy pleasure—and cost George and me nothing.

I have purposely refrained from mentioning the names of the many generous and hospitable people who entertained us in Norway, Sweden, and Denmark, but Mogens Lichtenberg should be an exception. He is the head of the National Travel Association of Denmark and he phoned us at the d'Angleterre in his official capacity.

We were out and we groaned when the porter handed us a message to call him. Sara had succumbed to The Bug the day after we arrived in Copenhagen. Lucy and George were just recovering from it. I could not afford to catch it as the other three had eaten up all the aureomycin pills, but the thought of crawling into bed for a few days was becoming more and more alluring.

So when I called Mr. Lichtenberg and he asked us to dine with him that evening, I explained our physical collapse with great politeness and begged to be excused. When Mogens Lichtenberg sets out to extend an official courtesy, however, he is not one to be pushed around with soft words, and the next thing I knew we had agreed to meet him downstairs at seven.

Lucy put on quite a temperamental scene about it. She had planned on going to bed early and why, she demanded, must she sit up all night talking to a wizened little old codger who undoubtedly spoke such bad English that she wouldn't be able to understand what he was talking about and who probably wouldn't say anything worth understanding anyway. Lucy has a very vivid imagination at such moments, and before she was through we were both in a despondent state of mind.

At seven a blond viking of a man, with a charm of manner and a smile that would have put him into the Big Time in Hollywood, met us in the lobby. He took Lucy by the arm, slipped her into the front seat of a brand-new Chrysler, and drove us to Nimbs in Tivoli.

"It seems to me," Lucy remarked, as we were left together for a moment while our host talked to the headwaiter, "that you sometimes say awfully mean things about people before you have any idea what you are talking about."

It is hard to describe Tivoli. Actually it is an amusement park set in the heart of the city, but so is the Grand Canyon an earth erosion in northern Arizona. Tivoli is an amusement park without the banana skins, the hot-dog stands, the canned jazz, the chewing-gum wrappers, discarded lunch boxes, torn newspapers, and all the other standard props of mass fun.

It is an amusement park in a Viennese operetta—an amusement park where symphony orchestras play against the undertones of roller coasters and the crowds move quietly along the graveled walks with never a wandering foot on the lush, green turf or a straying finger in the weedless flower beds.

Nor would the hardest-boiled Dane dream of dropping a newspaper or discarding a lunch box within the magic confines of Tivoli. In fact, one of the things that we could never understand about the Danes was what they did with their refuse. We watched them carefully, but never caught them disposing of any. They are inveterate smokers, for example, yet we never saw a cigarette or a cigar butt on the paths or the bordering grass. Possibly they swallow them.

We dined on a broad, raised terrace overlooking the park. No one wore evening clothes; but they would have been in harmony with the setting. The headwaiters bow no deeper in London's Carlton.

We watched the lights twinkling through the trees and the crowds moving slowly along the walks below us. On an open-air stage fifty yards away, a group of costumed dancers went through the routine of a minuet while we drank *snaps* and beer and ate crayfish tails and duck, cooked according to some secret formula known only to Lichtenberg and the headwaiter.

And while we ate and watched, Mogens talked about Denmark and then he began to speak of the Occupation during World War II. He told us of "undergrounds" and of the endless struggles of brave men who would not submit. At one point he seemed to have forgotten that we were there and to be living again through those years in the early forties. Below us the voices of the crowd were calm and cheerful and all about were lights and music and the sound of laughter. He broke off abruptly and apologized for his lapse.

We left the terrace and joined the slowly moving crowds.

20

More Copenhagen

I HAVE SPOKEN ABOUT THE SLOW DISINTEGRATION OF OUR desire for self-improvement which had been going on in all of us for some time past. An unseen borer had been eating away the solid core of our travel character until, like old apple trees, we had been reduced to hollow shells.

In the case of Lucy and Sara, even the shell of tourism was badly cracked. Faced with a plethora of castles, museums, churches and towers, they looked upon all of them with glazed, apathetic eyes. They had not yet reached the point of general refusal, but they could think of a dozen reasons for not visiting almost any specific place that one might mention.

As a result our Copenhagen coverage was spotty, but we would not have seen as much as we did had it not been for a Danish friend whose buoyant enthusiasm for all things Danish, coupled with rare personal charm, repeatedly broke down Sara's and Lucy's defenses. He was their Pied Piper and when he piped they tottered after him with little moaning sounds which were fortunately drowned by his music.

And then there were, of course, the places that we stumbled on accidentally. One morning I was hurrying down Amaliegade intent on keeping a twelve o'clock appointment and found myself in the great square which is bounded by Amalienborg Palace, just as the guard was being changed.

Being preoccupied with the problem of being late (a capital offense in Denmark) I was right in the middle of things before

I realized that something unusual was going on and that, from a Danish point of view at least, I was the most unusual thing about it. A policeman disentangled himself from the edge of the watching crowd, plunged into the ceremony and took me firmly by the arm. It was humiliating as well as alarming, for it never occurred to me that our destination could be anything but prison. To my surprise he led me to a spot in the shade of an archway.

"There can you see better please," he said. At that, he bowed stiffly and returned to his post. King Frederik V sat on his enormous bronze horse in the middle of the square and regarded this weakness of the modern constabulary with what looked like a slight sneer.

They were grand fellows, these guardsmen, in their light-blue trousers and their dark-blue coats glistening with polished buttons and crossed with white breast-straps. Enormous black busbies gave them a top-heavy look and also caused them to perspire freely. The lieutenants, who must have graduated from military college in their early teens, peered out like babes from underneath this martial millinery.

As usual in guard-changing, there was much marching and stopping and the shouting of fierce commands. I was particularly interested in the Danish method of getting troops off dead center. At the command "March," or its Danish equivalent, each soldier raised his right foot like a blind man groping for a stair and then set it down on the cobblestones with a bone-shattering crash after which he proceeded on his way with a kind of modified goose step. Quite possibly the first movement was designed to jar the busby firmly down over the eyes, thus avoiding any undignified accidents en route.

Sara and Lucy also visited one castle voluntarily. It was Rosenborg, where the Danish crown jewels are on display. That was a bait they could not resist. They stood fascinated before the great circular glass case and mentally tried on each and every piece.

George and I were equally interested from another angle. There was a rumor that if anyone so much as touched the case, bells and sirens would begin sounding off, the case would sink noiselessly through the floor, and the toucher would be whisked away to the dungeons.

All we had to do in order to put this chain reaction into operation was to reach across the iron guard-rail. It was like a "Fresh Paint" sign and we were both glad when we moved away.

Rosenborg Castle stands in the middle of a great park which, like Tivoli, occupies a large acreage in the center of Copenhagen. One approaches the castle along a broad drive flanked by lawns of such vicarious aristocracy that no weed has dared to raise its ugly head for almost four hundred years. Its great red towers rise above the ancient trees and within its walls are housed the collections of all Danish kings from Christian IV to Frederik VIII, who died in 1912.

Just what a "king's collection" might be was not explained to us, but it seemed to consist largely of the usual handouts which are made to rulers in the age-old hope that the donor will get something better in return.

It was an amazing conglomeration of the ugly and the valuable. No one had tried to hide his light under a bushel, the theory being that if one was going to bankrupt himself (or, more accurately speaking, his loyal subjects) making a royal gift, then let it be something that looked as expensive as it was—or, if possible, more so. These were the mink coats, television sets and refrigerators of an age unhampered by Congressional Committees.

Our voluntary visit to Rosenborg Castle was an exception, however, and for most of the enjoyable things that we saw in Copenhagen we were indebted to the bubbling enthusiasm of our Danish friend, who dispelled inertia and weariness as the sun melts a fog. He even succeeded in pacing us around the Elsinore circuit in one day, which under the circumstances was an amazing feat of personality.

A few miles north of Copenhagen, looking across the sound to Sweden, lies the town of Helsingør (Elsinore), and dominating its ancient buildings is Kronborg Castle. This would have posed no great problem had it not been for Shakespeare, who caused it to become all mixed up with Hamlet. As a result it has become a kind of international hoax, instead of an interesting sixteenth-century fortress adapted to shaking down unlucky vessels as they passed through the narrow sound between Sweden and Denmark within range of its stubby cannon.

Its builders prudently surrounded it with concentric walls of great thickness and with disagreeable-looking moats of great scumminess. Subterranean passages connect the castle to the walls which are hollow—a fact which somehow seemed disillusioning to us. In and below these walls the troops were quartered. They spent their lives, poor chaps, in these fortress dungeons, at once free men and prisoners.

We saw the stone bins in which their food was stored and the damp holes where it was cooked and where they ate it. Life could not have been healthy for the troops at Kronborg, but life below-stairs was cheap in those days.

Even among the mighty, however, the market was thin and its value could decline quickly. Further underground, below the troops and below the moat, were the real dungeons. In one place a long deep V had been cut into the rock. When the boys upstairs grew impatient with one of their associates, it was possible to jam the offender into the apex of the V, fasten an iron grille in front of him and leave him to play with the rats, or vice versa. Life was even cheaper in the subcellar.

On the return journey from Kronborg to Copenhagen, robust sight-seers stop off at Fredensborg and Frederiksborg, thus completing the Elsinore circuit. At least that is what the guidebooks say. When I have the pleasure of meeting Sydney Clark, the first question I want to ask him is whether he ever really covered Kronborg, Fredensborg and Frederiksborg in one day. We did.

Fredensborg is a royal residence placed in the midst of an exceptionally beautiful park. King Frederik and his suite were expected in a few days, so we were not allowed to go inside. As for the exterior, take all the idealized steel engravings and oil paintings of landscapes done between the years 1750 and 1850, stir them together, boil them down and the resulting essence is Fredensborg Park. We staggered through a mile or more of its tree-shaded paths and managed to get back to the car.

"Charming," said Lucy. "Home."

"Dreamy," said Sara, "I serve notice that I am going to be in bed within the hour."

Little did they know that ahead of them lay the biggest hurdle of all—Frederiksborg. This is the castle to end castles. It was built, like everything else around Copenhagen, by Christian IV and it must have been at the very peak and apex of his self-imposed building boom. Frederiksborg is so big that it is not really a castle, but rather a castle group rising from the surface of a lake. As we approached it over a causeway, silhouetted against the afternoon sun, it was something from an old fairy tale.

To Lucy and Sara it was something else. "Not another castle," they screamed hysterically.

Our Danish friend looked as fresh as he had when he had met us at the d'Angleterre that morning. "This should not be considered another castle," he assured them soothingly. On the other hand, he explained that to pass by Frederiksborg without having at least a look at it was like driving past the Taj Mahal with the shades down. His suggestion was that we dash in and just have a quick peek.

Taking a quick peek at Frederiksborg is like taking a scamper through the Ford plant or a squint at the Louvre. It is a complex of mammoth buildings, grand stairs, great halls, back halls and interminable passageways. A place where a king could lose his creditors and might even end up by losing himself.

Every inch of wall space in this huge pile is occupied by pictures, showcases, battle flags, and all the other oddments that a nation accumulates in the course of a lifetime in much the same way as an individual—only there is no one constantly nagging at a nation to know when it is going "to weed out some of this junk."

As we have said, our host was an enthusiast on the subject of Danish history and Danish tradition. He reacted to his surroundings like a well-trained foxhound and fled in full cry down the corridors, through the great halls and up and down the grand stairs. Lucy, Sara, George and I followed as best we could with no cries of "Tallyho" or any desire to be in at the death. Our only thought was that if we ever lagged behind and became separated, we might spend the rest of our lives lost among the memorabilia of Denmark.

Then we went through a final oak door and, quite unexpectedly, found ourselves in the great courtyard. Our friend's energy seemed to have been stimulated by this last run. "It's a shame you couldn't have taken more time," he said, looking at his wrist watch, "but I guess we'll have to hurry if you are going out to dinner at seven."

We had read somewhere in Sydney Clark that the service in Copenhagen restaurants is the slowest in Europe. This interested us. Having tested Norway and Sweden, it seemed to us that Sydney was setting an impossibly high standard. As usual, however, he was right. Eating in Copenhagen is a gastronomic delight, but you do not go in for it as a dilettante—you have to work at it.

We were always deceived at the start. On our entering a

restaurant, the headwaiter would be at our elbow before the last person was through the door. A swarm of waiters helped us into our chairs and adjusted the table silver a mite this way or that, giving the feeling that the success of this meal meant a great deal to the entire staff.

The second headwaiter then distributed enormous menu cards containing hundreds of unintelligible items, gave the table a last paternal once-over as if to assure himself that things were as near perfection as humanly possible, then bowed and left us. We were now as much alone as if we had been parachuted into the Canadian wilderness.

After half an hour, we began clutching at the sleeves of passing waiters. Of course, this merely caused them to spill whatever they might be carrying and never brought a flicker of recognition into their stolid faces. Eventually either George or I, spurred to boldness by Sara and Lucy, would round up one of the two headwaiters.

These gentlemen were always upset to find that we were upset. They would, of course, take our order in person. And what would we have to drink? We would start, let us say, with a *snaps* and beer?

At this point, the headwaiter would bark and in less time than it takes a prestidigitator to pull a parrot cage from under his opera cloak, the *snaps* and beer were in front of us.

The human mind has little ability to remember pain. We were immediately serene, sipping our drinks contentedly while Lucy and Sara commented on the charming personality of the headwaiter and declared that they could not wait to get their teeth into *Hummerskaller fyldt med stuvede Asparges med Dild, derpaa Hummarkødet maskeret med Dildsauce, glaceret,* a dish which we had been assured would throw us into gastronomic ecstasies.

Then the drinks would be finished and for fifteen or twenty minutes we would make amiable conversation which gradually trailed off, as hunger took over, until it became obvious that in another minute George was about to lose control. At precisely the breaking point, however, the swinging doors would always fly open and two waiters would come hurrying in bearing enormous covered platters. As we ate the delicious things which they contained, we wondered why Americans were so impatient.

By the time we had swallowed the last mouthful two hours had passed. This was concession enough to Continental easygoingness. We would begin to look around for our waiter with an idea of paying the check and moving on—but all waiters had completely vanished.

Eventually the captain would reappear through the swinging doors, eyes downcast, and wearing that look of troubled preoccupation which members of his craft always assume when you are trying to attract their attention. One of us would get up and trot along beside him, explaining that we had an appointment and must, therefore, leave immediately. He would nod absently as a man might who has just received bad news from home and then disappear through swinging doors on the other side of the room. Fifteen minutes later, George's temper would erupt like Old Faithful. It went off in two sequences. During the first, he pounded on the table, glared savagely and declared that he was an American. During the second phase, he would rise from the table and stalk angrily from the room followed by the rest of us. This maneuver usually worked. The headwaiter would appear from behind a curtain, or wherever he had been hiding, and we would settle up at the door. Once the act misfired, however, and we found ourselves out on the street without having paid for our dinner. Being basically honest, this involved coming back and doing our exit all over again, which was undignified.

We were invited to visit the manor house of Nysø in south Zealand by the charming young couple who are fortunate enough to live there.

174

Accompanied by our Danish friend, we drove down from Copenhagen late one afternoon and on the way stopped at Vallø, a turreted castle surrounded by a double moat. This romantic building is occupied by a maximum of eleven spinsters of unchallenged aristocracy. Just as in the United States boys are sometimes entered at birth in certain preparatory schools, so is a Danish nobleman apt to enter his daughter in Vallø. At the same time he puts up a small sum of money. I understood that it is the equivalent of a thousand dollars. If the daughter marries, he forfeits the entrance fee. If Cupid bypasses her, however, she may enter Vallø at the proper time—and when there is an opening. In view of the fact that most Danish girls marry and gladly forfeit their entrance fees, the endowment fund is said to be enormous.

A cobbled causeway now spans the two moats and enters the building through an archway leading to a central court. Here at one time stood the portcullis. Now peacocks strut about the open entrance selecting morsels from between the cobbles.

The ladies of the castle are in no sense voluntary prisoners. Good taste, however, imposes certain limits on human conduct. For this reason, the ladies may drive abroad whenever they wish *but* never in an automobile. While we waited, watching the golden light of the setting sun playing on the ancient bricks, an octogenarian led two horses across a stable yard on our right. He backed them into the shafts of an open landau and another man of lesser rank harnessed them.

Soon the carriage emerged. The horses trotted sedately across the causeway and through the entrance tunnel into the inner court. For sheer haughtiness, the coachman might have qualified as a doorman for the Stork Club. Our Danish friend explained that because the original grant of the castle was from the Queen, the coachmen at Vallø were entitled to wear red on their collars— a statement which he seemed to feel explained everything.

An elderly man and woman came out of a door in the arched entrance, entered the landau and the whole equipage trotted smartly past the place where we were standing. We felt as if we should be wearing smocks and pulling our forelocks.

From Vallø we drove south on the back roads which are the joy of Danish motoring. They took us through forests of beech and oak devoid, as usual, of underbrush. These were part of great landed estates—estates which have been considerably diminished during recent years by the impact of social reform.

From time to time we passed thatched gamekeepers' cottages tucked away in the woods. This was the kind of country where, in the fairy stories, the handsome young prince or the king is always losing himself and coming on a charcoal burner's hut. It is the country of witches, princesses with overgrown blond hair and benign dwarfs—a country which made Hans Christian Andersen seem more like an historian than a romancer.

To anyone conditioned to ranch-house developments in the United States the great manor houses of Denmark come as an agreeable shock. These Danish estates are still occupied for the most part by the families who have dwelt in them for centuries. Nothing has been changed, yet most of them have been so well maintained both inside and out that although the visitor has the feeling of age, it is age which belongs to the present as well as to the past. The furniture gleams unmarred in the candlelight. Apparently Danish liquor leaves no rings and Danish servants do not run carpet sweepers into table legs. The ancient portraits beam down from the walls, not as strangers glowering across the centuries, but as contemporaries glad to be in on the party.

Outside, the turf of the lawns reflects generations of loving care. No underbrush chokes the bases of the ancient trees and what becomes of their dead limbs is a secret known only to the Danes.

The consumption of food is a major industry in Copenhagen from swanky
d'Angleterre's sidewalk café to the fish market. (*Danish Information Office*)

Denmark never allows its settings to become frayed or shopworn

Den Gamle By—Århus
(*Danish Information Office*)

House in which Hans Christian Andersen was born

They call it the Paris of the North, but Copenhagen is just Copenhagen—which should be enough for anyone

They were haughty fellows, these guards-men. (*Danish Information Office*)

A country of thatched-roof granges splotched
with moss (*Danish Information Office*)

—and moated castle from a childhood dream

Jutland—a land of contented abundance—its hands
folded across its stomach (*Danish Information Office*)

—where affairs move slowly
(*Danish Information Office*)

—and all things are sturdy and well
preserved. (*Danish Information Office*)

—while Pop brings home the bacon.
(Danish International Office.)

Mother just pushes the apples around

—or in them. (*Danish Information Office*)

Young and old, rich and poor, they are all on bicycles

Nyhavn—where at night the lights from the sailors' bars shine on the gleaming sides of ships

Here at Nysø, the sculptor Thorvaldsen and Hans Christian Andersen used to visit, twenty-five years before our Civil War was dreamed of, and it was here that Andersen wrote "Ole Lukoie" and "The Bell."

Today one enters, just as he did, through a low-arched passage in a long outbuilding. A hundred yards away, at the end of the cobbled approach, the two-storied house, with its high-gabled roof, stands like a host waiting to welcome his visitors. Like almost all Danish manor houses, it was once moated, but the moats are now filled in except at either end where swans paddle sedately among the lilies.

Bicycles, churches, moated castles, bronze statues stumbled upon in unexpected places, open sandwiches, twisted towers, flower markets, traffic policemen waving white-gantleted gloves in aesthetic rhythm, the harbor and the little bronze mermaid, sidewalk cafés and the twinkling lights of Tivoli, museums, fish markets, Nyhavn, where the lights from the sailors' bars flicker on the black sides of the ships, Royal Copenhagen porcelain, baroque buildings, crayfish tails, and the noiseless, ceaseless passage of bicycles—these are the ingredients. Put them all together, stir well—and you have Copenhagen.

2 1

Funen

WE LEFT COPENHAGEN AS UNWILLINGLY AS WE HAD
Stockholm. George and I were also oppressed by secret misgivings.
This loop that we were about to make around the Danish countryside had been our own special idea, something we had thought up
all by ourselves. We knew in advance just where the blame would
lie if the results did not measure up to our sales talk.

The broad road to Korsør rolled westward between rows of
newly planted lindens. At Korsør we were to take the ferry to
Funen, Denmark's "middle island." Sara and George were engaged
in a routine quarrel about the car windows. If we had had nothing
else to occupy us on the entire trip, the adjustment of the windows
would have provided an unfailing source of spirited argument. It
also provided a sensitive barometer of nerve pressures. An old-timer
could have told just how well everyone had slept the night before
merely by listening to the battle of the windows.

Sara and Lucy, who always offered a united front in this matter,
insisted that, by twisting the two little half windows until they
stood out from the car like elephant's ears, it was possible to let
down the large front windows without causing a draft in the back
seat.

Whether or not there was anything to this theory was of minor
importance. The real difficulty arose from the fact that when the
little windows were at right angles to the car, they set up a roar
like Victoria Falls.

George was very sensitive to noises and he considered this
situation intolerable. It was his theory that a pleasant circulation
could only be achieved by sliding open the long side windows in

178

the rear of the car. Why he stuck to this contention I do not know, as it obviously produced a violent draft on the back of everyone's neck. Perhaps he did not believe it, but merely used it as a counter-irritant.

I reserved for myself the role of roving troublemaker, throwing my weight where I thought it would do the most harm and occasionally, on days when the digestive mechanism was not working too well, thinking up bizarre combinations which were bound to alienate everyone.

Roskilde Cathedral lay on our route to the ferry. Roskilde is the Westminster Abbey of Denmark or, as George put it more crudely, the cold-storage center for Danish royalty. Here, according to the books, lay the remains of that doughty father of kings, Harold Bluetooth. There was something forthright and frank about the name which attracted me to the man. He was obviously the sort of person who would never have permitted his subjects to hang false, hypocritical tags on him like Harold the Good, or Harold the Magnificent. There he was, take him or leave him—blue tooth and all.

I had a secret desire to pay homage to such fearless honesty. Under the circumstances, however, I hesitated even to suggest a short stopover at Roskilde. In their present mood, I knew just how Lucy and Sara would react to the idea of further sight-seeing.

So when we arrived at the Cathedral, I merely said, in the most casual way, that I wanted to stick my nose inside for a half-second. I admitted frankly that it was a crazy whim, the kind of thing that no one in his sane mind would do, but I asked them to humor me for a brief instant.

Of course, *they* were not to come. No one need move. They could sit in the car and look out over the rolling fields to the blue waters of Roskilde Fjord or up at the great white clouds which moved so majestically above it—or, they could just sit in the car.

To my surprise, Lucy and Sara were more indignant than if I had commanded them to inspect the Cathedral from nave to belfry. They said that under no circumstances did they propose to be pushed aside. This was *their* trip as much as mine, and if Roskilde Cathedral was good enough for me, it certainly seemed as if it might be good enough for them.

For the next hour we walked through its brick-trimmed, ornate interior, peering through wrought-iron screens and prowling around the intricately carved sarcophagi of dead kings and queens. I was so stunned by the unpredictability of the female mind that I forgot to look for the last resting place of Harold Bluetooth.

Lucy and Sara were charmed. Roskilde was their discovery and it raised their spirits immensely. When we finally emerged again into the sunlight, the only traces of bad humor remaining were directed at me for trying to deprive them of such an exhilarating experience. Roskilde taught me something.

At Korsør, we took a great ferry to Nyborg on the island of Funen. We lunched aboard on—believe it or not—raw eggs and beef tea. It was such a fantastic combination that when I saw it on the menu, my mind went back to Roskilde and I ordered it as a matter of scientific research rather than with anticipation. I said that it was just a crazy idea which I was sure to regret and insisted that everyone else go for a sounder dish. Lucy and Sara were feeling their new-found independence, however, and immediately ordered raw eggs and beef tea. I begged them not to, but they hooted me down and begged me in turn to leave them free at least to choose their own food. When the concoction arrived, they raved about it.

Apparently I had stumbled on something much bigger than I realized. Unfortunately, it was a bit late in the game.

A large-scale map of Denmark gives the impression that some one dropped it when it was young and shattered it rather badly.

The eastern section is a long peninsula shooting north from Germany and almost sealing off the Baltic. This was very properly named Jut-land. To the east of Jutland a series of islands form stepping-stones to Sweden. The two biggest ones are Funen and Zealand. Copenhagen lies on the easternmost bulge of Zealand, looking across the sound toward Swedish Malmö.

Funen, the middle island, is a roly-poly affair not much more than seventy-five kilometers in diameter. Odense, its principal city, sits in the center with roads radiating from it in all directions causing it to look, on the map, like a dozing spider.

Odense was ancient in 1086 when King Kanute was killed there, and in England one could still pick up souvenirs on the battlefield at Hastings. Ordinarily such venerability would be enough for any small city to cope with, but the antiquity of Odense has been smothered by the fact that it is the birthplace of Hans Christian Andersen, that strange, awkward, bedeviled man who wanted to write novels and plays, but immortalized himself with fairy tales.

We found the house where he is alleged to have been born, without difficulty as all street signs point to it regardless of where one happens to be. It is a one-storied, red-tiled bandbox of a place standing at the intersection of two twisting lanes. Whether or not Andersen was really born there appears to be a matter of some doubt, but that, apparently, is a minor point which bothers no one.

The little house snuggles confidently against an imposing museum and the two buildings are stuffed with an amazing collection of Anderseniana. It is hard, however, to become interested in an author's baby shoes and stovepipe hat regardless of how much one may admire his work—and we did want to get to Svendborg, where we could settle down for two days with nothing to do. The woman at the door who had sold us our tickets, looked at us in amazement as we hurried out. The Danes are thrifty-minded and like their customers to get their money's worth.

People are apt to think of Denmark as a flatland. Some of it is, but much more of it is rolling, lush, and beautiful. In the amber light of evening, the low hills seemed to glow with a special radiance of their own. Big windmills dotted the horizon, their broad arms turning slowly. The thatched roofs of the barns were mottled with green moss. Wheat and barley stood in sheaves in the fields. Ancient trees lined the roads. It was a world in which all was settled —a world which sought no change.

As we neared Svendborg, the familiar cold sweat of apprehension gathered on my forehead, for this was the place which George and I had selected as the ideal spot to recuperate after Copenhagen. On a trip like ours a three-night stand represented a major decision.

Sydney Clark had sold us on the idea. He had become quite lyrical about Svendborg, referring to it as "a temple of tourism," "Denmark's center for the sport of yachting," and "the Danish Cowes." I don't quite know what we expected the Christiansminde Hotel to be like. Personally, I had built up a picture of a long, white-pillared structure facing an esplanade, on the other side of which were the blue waters of the harbor—waters with gleaming yachts dancing on their surface. I had peopled the grounds of the hotel and the esplanade with gay, fashionably dressed crowds dodging about in sports roadsters and waving tennis rackets at one another. That was my idea of a Danish Cowes, a rather positive concept perhaps, in view of the fact that I had never seen the English one.

I was as nonplused as the others, therefore, when the Christiansminde turned out to be a rather somber-looking, brown stucco affair with a large gravel parking space in the rear, devoid of sports roadsters and with not a waving tennis racket in sight. In fact, there was no one in sight. Through the trees we caught a glimpse of water, and at the foot of the hill below the hotel was a little dock beside which a few small sailboats bobbed restlessly.

Inside, the general impression was dark-brown and stuffy. A Danish family eyed us suspiciously from one corner. They were neither gay nor fashionably dressed.

Louisa took charge at that point and immediately things became brighter. Louisa was the soul of the Christiansminde and the dynamo which made it go. She was a five-foot powerhouse who regarded everything as excruciatingly funny and appeared to consider each detail of her sordid and endless toil as a colorful adventure.

A morose young man was sharing the front desk with Louisa when we entered, but she quickly shouldered him out of the way and assumed full charge of our registration. Then she gave us our keys, seized two of the biggest suitcases, and romped upstairs with them, laughing.

We had watched many people romp upstairs with our luggage, but never before had anyone laughed during the process.

Later we found her helping in the dining room. After dinner it was Louisa who served coffee in the lounge. When I went to telephone, it was Louisa who manned the switchboard, and when I entered my room after breakfast the following morning, it was Louisa who was making the bed. I asked her where I might get my suit pressed. It was a foolish question. Louisa reached for it, overcome with laughter.

Whenever in the years ahead I feel put-upon, tired, hounded, and harassed—whenever the world looks dun-colored and uninteresting —I am resolved to think of Louisa, laughing her way through seventeen different jobs in the Christiansminde Hotel at Svendborg.

In spite of Louisa, I could not take too optimistic a view of things. A cold wind rattled the windows and the low, gray clouds foretold rain. But Roskilde had put me in possession of a powerful new weapon. The following morning while we were enjoying an excellent breakfast, I said all the unpleasant things I could think of about Svendborg and its surroundings. The reaction was immediate. The more I bemoaned the situation and the more critical I became, the more Sara and Lucy cheered up and declared Svendborg and the Christiansminde, in particular, to be one of their favorite spots.

When I thought the situation was in hand, I went out on the terrace and sought a secluded place to do some writing. In front of me an iron fawn, painted olive drab, lay placidly in a bed of brilliant red flowers. I began to relax. There are times when it is good to be alone.

At that moment, Lucy and Sara sauntered out onto the long terrace. Although it was quite deserted they selected a table three or four feet away, where they chatted happily and loudly about the kind of clothes they would bring if they ever took exactly the same trip again. After a time I moved into the lounge.

There were only two or three people there, none of whom showed any signs of life. I had just begun to settle down again when the aroma from a cigar of tremendous strength attacked the membranes of my nose, causing it to twitch violently. I looked up to find that it was being smoked by a particularly chic Danish lady of middle age. Sara and Lucy came in complaining of the wind. I put my writing away.

In addition to medieval cities and villages, Denmark is generously sprinkled with ancient castles and manor houses and there is a special concentration of them on the island of Funen. Through the kindness of mutual friends, we had been invited to visit Glorup a few miles northeast of Svendborg, which is one of the most beautiful and best preserved of the Danish manor houses.

It is built around four sides of a cobbled court and approached through a magnificent avenue of lindens. On the north side it is pierced by an archway which leads into the inner court. After a long debate, we drove the car through it. It is so hard to know whether automobiles are supposed to enter the inner court-yards of historic Danish houses. To have made a mistake would have been like riding a horse into someone's front hall.

Our charming young host and hostess were on hand to greet us. From the cordiality of their reception, one might have supposed that we were the four people in the world whom they most wanted to see instead of four strangers from the States come to shatter the calm of their Sunday routine.

Through the broad windows of the living room we looked down vistas of lawn, bordered by ancient trees. To the west was a small lake which at one time must have formed part of a defensive moat. Inside, the house was so big, so lovely, so filled with the graceful trappings of yesterday, so peopled with the ghosts of aristocracy, that I felt, suddenly, like the interloper that I was and developed a tendency to catch my feet under the legs of chairs.

On the grounds of Glorup stands the castle of Rygaard which, for sheer antiquity, makes the manor house look like a newcomer. Built in 1530, its spiral stairway is made of great, triangular wooden blocks laid one on another like the panels of an open fan. Our host pointed out to us that it ascended clockwise in order, he explained, to free the sword arm of the person defending the stairs from above.

Later that afternoon, after we had left our hospitable friends, we visited Egeskov. This was the first completely moated castle we had seen. We came to it when the low August sun was bathing every-thing with yellow light. The unruffled waters of the broad moat reflected every detail of the red walls, the pepperbox corner tower and the square, step-like dormers. The only concession to modernity was the replacement of the old drawbridge with a stone causeway.

On our side of the moat were acres of flower gardens, beautifully clipped hedges ten to twelve feet high and, as a background, giant old lindens glowing in the unreal light. It was like walking backwards through time into the pages of a childhood romance.

As a symbol of the continuity of human affairs, the grounds of Egeskov appeared to be a center for lovers. We kept stumbling on them at every twist of the hedge-bordered paths and even found them embedded in the hedges. It became positively embarrassing, yet it would be hard to be anything but a lover in such a place.

We drove away through a broad avenue of lindens, so old and so thick that only a green, watery light filtered through to the cobbled road below—and so, happily, back to Louisa and supper.

There are many islands to the south of Funen. On Monday, George and I put the Plymouth on a little flatboat ferry and took it over to Taasinge where it was in a world seldom troubled by automobiles.

We drove slowly along the narrow, twisting lanes, stopping every few moments to take pictures of the low, whitewashed, half-timbered farmhouses and barns, their thatched roofs blotched with moss. The farmers, who had been confronted with these settings since infancy and regarded them with the traditional attitude of familiarity, watched us with incredulous astonishment.

Our gasoline was running low. There were not many towns on Taasinge, and we were relieved to find a gasoline pump standing beside a blacksmith's shop on the edge of a village. The blacksmith was a startling fellow with a leather apron and an unbelievably dirty face, gnarled and twisted like a desert piñon. His teeth, however, were the most remarkable part of his features. They just made the plural by one and both were colored a dark blue. We stared at him realizing that here, on this remote little island, we had stumbled on a direct descendant of our friend Harold Bluetooth.

We were going to need close to fifteen gallons. Now, in Scandinavia, gasoline is sold by the liter and there are approximately 3.8 liters to a gallon. Furthermore, gasoline costs about eighty-four öre per liter. Figure it out for yourself and you will have to admit that we were about to invest quite a few öre.

The blacksmith was a frugal man to whom an öre was an öre regardless of which side of the counter he stood. As the liters began to flash by on the dial of the gasoline pump, he looked more and more distressed and finally shook his head and turned off the pump. We had purchased twenty liters costing approximately 1,680 öre and that was enough for any man. It may also have crossed his prudent mind that it might be just as well not to extend further credit until he saw the color of the stranger's gold.

His thoughts on these matters being undoubtedly complex and he being unable to speak a word of English, we had some difficulty in arriving at a satisfactory understanding. We finally took out all our money and laid it on the front seat of the car, thus indicating that we wanted the gas tank filled even though it caused our last öre to disappear into the pocket of his leather apron.

He poured in another twenty liters and stopped again. This time he smiled, shrugged his shoulders and hung up the hose. Even if we *could* pay for it, we had reached a point in extravagance where sensible men should begin to think of the general good of the community and put a stop to such insanity. It was hard to argue a philosophical point of this kind in sign language.

Finally, a native of the village came sauntering by who understood a little English. We explained to him that, cost what it might, we wanted to fill the tank. He talked earnestly and at length with the blacksmith, apparently explaining to him that the latter's duty to his family transcended his public responsibilities. Reluctantly, Mr. Bluetooth removed the hose from its holder, and filled us up to a total of fifty-seven liters. We left him counting almost five thousand öre and gesticulating to his friend. His ancestor would have been proud of him.

My hair had been hanging further over my collar each day until, for the last week, I began to look like pictures of Columbus at the court of Ferdinand and Isabella. I inquired of Mr. Hansen, who seemed to officiate at the desk of the Christiansminde when Louisa was occupied elsewhere, if there was a barber in town who could give me the kind of a haircut to which I was accustomed. It was rather difficult to explain to him, in my then condition, just what that might have been. It would have simplified things if I could have told him that any kind of a haircut which differed from the one *he* was wearing would be more or less satisfactory.

He was a friendly sort of chap, however, and finally phoned a barber with whom he held a long conversation in Danish. Here was a man, he told me, who could not speak English, but who was prepared to cut my hair in exactly the style I desired.

Half an hour later, I found myself in the barber chair making motions with my hands to indicate just what I wanted to accomplish. At first he seemed puzzled, then I saw the light of understanding come into his face. "Like Hansen," he shouted triumphantly, and seizing me by the shoulders, he pulled me back into the chair and went to work.

There was no use struggling. In fact it would have been dangerous, for this man operated in a kind of creative frenzy. He finally finished in a blaze of electric clippers and began to talk excitedly in Danish. I concluded that he was asking for my approval and I automatically nodded. He nodded back and poured over my head a double handful of liquid soap, with which he created an enormous globe of suds while I remained seated in the barber chair. When he had, in some amazing manner, removed this without the aid of water he again began to talk.

This time I took no chances. I said, "No, *nein*, nay." He nodded understandingly, selected a bottle from the shelf beside us and poured on several handfuls of strong scent. Again he leaned down and fired a burst of Danish into my ear. I tried to rise from the chair, but he pushed me back, nodded, and seized an electric drier which immediately fluffed up my hair so that it looked like a Fiji Islander's.

He pointed to it reproachfully. This time I shouted "Yes" for no other reason than to see what would happen. Obviously I could not go out on the street like that. It was the signal for him to saturate my hair with oil. Then he combed it neatly in the manner of Hitler, threw off the big apron with a flourish and bowed deeply.

We left Svendborg on Tuesday morning at eight-thirty in a driving rain and a gale of wind, bound for Faaborg, twenty-five miles to the west. There we were to take the ferry to Mommark in Jutland, just north of the German border.

The wind had whipped up quite a sea and our big ferry floundered a bit as we drew away from the shore, its thrashing bow throwing sheets of salt water over the forward deck. Behind us, Faaborg was a long line of pink and red roofs with the square belfry of the ancient church rising protectingly above them. Behind the town lay a low range of hills, marked in pastel squares of green and brown and crowned with a purple forest.

2 2

South Jutland

SØNDERBORG IS THE FIRST CITY THAT ONE COMES TO IN
South Jutland after leaving the ferry at Mommark. We lunched
there, looking out across the narrow harbor at a row of aged yellow
and pink warehouses and watching the gulls maneuver tirelessly
against a gale which ripped the tops off the little waves and flung
them at the corner of the Alhambra Hotel.

We were all agreed that we wanted a light lunch. It was a
decision we were constantly reaching, but although it sounds like
a simple project, it was one which we never seemed able to carry
out. The only dish on the Alhambra's menu which remotely
promised to meet our requirement was an omelet. At the end of a
half-hour a tired-looking waiter staggered in with four omelets, each
the size of a mature salmon and stuffed to bursting with all the
farm products of Denmark. Between them they must have represented a week's output of an active barnyard, working on three
shifts.

We ate until we could not push down another mouthful, then
headed southwest as best we could through gently rolling country
which flattened out as we neared the sea until it assumed the
enormous horizons of a Wyoming landscape. The wind, with the
heavy playfulness of a Newfoundland puppy, tried to shoulder
us off the road and threw weather at us so fast that one minute
we were running under blue skies and the next were bucking a
lashing rain with ceiling zero.

Sydney Clark had warned us that no visit to North Slesvig is
complete without a stopover at Tønder and Møgeltønder near the

German border. This fitted in with a morbid desire of Lucy and Sara to see the border itself. They had bypassed noble cathedrals, brushed aside historic castles and pooh-poohed several thousand acres of art galleries, but they yearned to see the invisible line that separated Germany from Jutland.

Sydney was right on both recommendations. Tønder looked like a stage-set for a seventeenth-century German play. Its crooked little streets wriggled off from the central square in all directions and were lined with crooked little houses whose tiled roofs came down so low that one could rest one's elbow on the eaves while talking to a friend. Most of them had bay windows filled with flowers, from behind which the inhabitants could maintain a ceaseless vigil over practically nothing.

Møgeltønder is only a few miles from Tønder, and one must proceed slowly or risk overshooting it. Toy brick houses line its single street, hiding behind a double row of trees trimmed after the manner of French poodles. We stopped long enough to lay in the usual supply of postal cards and pressed on to the German border at Rudebøl.

Two bored-looking Danish soldiers stopped us a hundred yards from the barrier, apparently to eliminate any chance of our taking a flying start and crashing into Germany in a cloud of splinters. They permitted us to walk to the line, heads bent against the gale which was threatening to blow the village of Rudebøl into the North Sea, guards, barrier and all.

Lucy and Sara leaned on the barrier pole and gazed fascinatedly across the street into Germany. Their immediate foreground was a drab, one-story building. Its door opened. A bored-looking German youth in uniform appeared in the doorway, returned their stare for a few minutes, then shut the door with difficulty against the wind. We turned the car around, thanked the friendly Danes and headed north along the west coast toward Ribe.

The trim neatness which we had come to associate with Denmark suddenly vanished and then, after a few miles, the houses did likewise. It was a country of broad plains, most of them below sea level, with the raised road running parallel to a huge dike which stood between us and the sea. The fields were divided by deep ditches, instead of fences, which were spanned at intervals by wooden bridges with gates in the middle—and scattered over the landscape to the horizon were herds of steers and thousands of fat cows and great flocks of overfed sheep.

About twenty miles up the coast we pulled abreast of the island of Rømø, which is connected with the mainland by a ten-mile causeway—just why we never discovered. We were determined to pass up nothing in this extraordinary country, however, so we drove across it, bucking a gale from the North Sea which piled the waves against the sloping grass banks on either side of the road and drenched the car with spray.

On the seaward coast of Rømø is the father of all beaches. Mogens Lichtenberg had told us that on a normal day it is a mile from the dunes to the water's edge. Now the gale had blown the sea up the beach almost to the grass. A mile out we could see the white walls of tumbling water which broke, then boiled and foamed across the beach to the wheels of the car. It was no place for casual bathing.

Back on the causeway with the wind behind us, we half-sailed, half-motored to the mainland and resumed our journey to Ribe.

It would never have occurred to us to visit Ribe had it not been for Sydney Clark. But who could resist statements like these:

"I will say without reservation that it is one of the supreme small towns of Europe in its medieval beauty . . . It has been called a bit of Elizabethan England brought by the tides to the marshes of Jutland, but one could quite as fairly say that England's picture towns were brought by the tide from Denmark.

"Ribe is one of those towns deserted by the sea and left to the mercies of passing time. One finds them all over Europe, for example Bruges in Belgium, Pisa in Italy and, for that matter, Tønder, its near neighbor to the south. Once they were all of importance as seaports, but the sea receded and silt filled their harbors. Each became the widow of a dead coast and was left to dream out its days and grow old graciously."

That sounded to us as if Sydney might be laying it on a bit, and George and I had our fingers crossed as we approached the town over the marshy flatlands. Happily, however, it was everything that he had said—and more. There is a bit of Ribe in every Danish country town, but here it was almost simon-pure.

In Denmark we had again run afoul of our old nocturnal tormentor, the *dyne*. Somehow these Danish *dyner* had seemed easier to cope with than their Norwegian cousins. Perhaps we were becoming more adaptable. Perhaps the nip of late August nights made them more bearable. Perhaps it was sheer exhaustion.

Whatever the reason, we had become almost reconciled to them until at the Riberhus, our neat little hotel in Ribe, we ran head on into something new in *dyner*—a monstrous affair which must have weighed over ten pounds. On the first night I dreamed that, while working in a coal mine, the thing caved in on top of me. Self-preservation caused me to hurl the *dyne* to the floor, after which I spent the rest of the night shivering under my raincoat.

On the second night I solved the problem by unbuttoning the envelope of my *dyne*, removing the ten pounds of comforter, and replacing it with my own body. By piling all clothing within reach on top of this Danish sleeping bag, I passed a reasonably comfortable night.

The following morning I took up with the porter the question of obtaining some blankets. Unfortunately he spoke no English whatsoever, and taking things up can be difficult under those circumstances. After some delay he became convinced that I was

complaining about the food and called the chef, who quite errone-
ously fancied himself as a linguist. I tried to explain with words and
sign language that the food was excellent (although perhaps there
was too much of it) and that what I wanted was blankets—blankets
such as soldiers use in the field. I gave a graphic pantomime of
soldiers using blankets in the field. The chef's face lit up. He led
me to a window and pointed to a time-scarred building at the end
of the street which later turned out to be the railroad station. Then
he shook hands violently and retired to his kitchen.

It takes some time for a casual visitor to realize that Ribe is not
a stage-set, but a real town where people marry, have babies, quarrel,
and make their living (in spite of all the odds against it) just as
they do in less spectacular places.

We were seeing it at its best. The relatively few tourists who
penetrate to this picturesque backwater had been blown home by
the first gales of fall. Ribe was putting on its show for us alone,
which is the only way to see it properly. A place like this should
be a national secret and it should be made an act of treason to
write about it.

On the following day we wandered for hours through the twisting medieval streets and alleys, staring unbelievingly at the half-
timbered houses which must have been standing when the Pilgrim
Fathers were still raising money for the "Mayflower." We gaped at
the storks' nests built on platforms obligingly placed on the ridge
poles by the house owners. We peered into the dark shop of the
butter-barrel maker and took colored pictures of the postman in his
red coat and the milk wagon with the spigots on the back where
the housewives of Ribe gather with pitchers, mugs and little buckets
to exchange the gossip of the day.

We even found a town crier complete with bell. He was not a
particularly picturesque-looking character and we did not know

what he was crying, but he was the only town crier we had ever seen and we valued him accordingly. Sara and Lucy are very sensitive about such things. They insisted that it would be bad taste to take his picture as if he were an animal or a statue and would make him think that Americans were coarse people. They argued this point until the crier planted himself in front of the camera and posed. Their disillusionment was complete when, after the first shot, he smiled broadly and said: "Do it again."

George became so excited by it all that he lost his passport. As we were finishing lunch the waiter told us with bulging eyes that the Chief of Police would like a word with us at the desk. A message like that brings out the latent criminal in every man. Resisting the temptation to slip out through the kitchen, however, we forced ourselves to go to the front office. There we found a magnificent man full of old-world courtesy. He said that he had had the honor to collect the passport of the gentleman from a gutter and if we would extend to him the courtesy of accompanying him to the police station, he would be pleased to deliver it in person.

Later we visited the Post Office, probably one of the most remarkable buildings of its kind in the world. The entrance is through a cobbled courtyard between impressive gateposts, then up a circular stairway in a brick tower. On the second floor we found ourselves in a kind of official palace surrounded by wrought-iron grillwork, gleaming brass signs, leaded glass windows, and carved woodwork. A cathedral hush hung over everything.

A clerk, in one of the scarlet coats which make the postmen of Jutland look like MFH's, appeared through a carved oak doorway and asked us what our pleasure would be. Had he asked us to step in and have a drink, it would not have been surprising. His associates looked us over and then continued their careful sorting of the mail.

Finally, however, after we had walked up one winding alley

and down another for a matter of hours, even Ribe began to suffer from too much familiarity. Storks' nests no longer affected our blood pressure—an old mill, fed by a tree-shaded millstream, appearing suddenly in the middle of a block, excited no comment—the little V-shaped mirrors attached to the outside of all living-room windows, giving the occupants an unobstructed view in both directions, became standard equipment to us—wavy roof lines and half-timbered houses, whose walls followed the curve of the narrow street, failed to bring a camera out of its case.

We were temporarily saturated with the old and the quaint and staggered back to the Riberhus to fall exhausted on our excellent, modern beds.

That afternoon we motored north to the city of Esbjerg, Denmark's biggest North Sea port. There we took a ferry to the island of Fanø. We had heard much about Fanø—its great summer hotels, its magnificent beach where one can drive twenty cars abreast (which struck us as a stupid form of motoring), and the village of Sønderho where the tourists flock to see its tiny houses, its colorful folk costumes and its beautiful women. It all sounded like a good kind of a place to recover from an overdose of antiquity.

It was late in the season, however—the twenty-seventh of August. The smartest of summer hotels have a tendency to frumpiness as soon as the boards go up, and unoccupied beaches have a hostile look which increases in direct ratio to their size. Instead of gay hotels and casinos, we found what seemed to us a rather hideous ganglion of shoddy-looking buildings, all closed. We could not even find the road to the beach so, somewhat frustrated, we drove to Sønderho at the opposite end of the island for a look at the tiny houses, the colorful costumes and the beautiful women.

The tiny houses were there, but the only signs of life that we saw among them were a butcher boy pulling a child's express cart, an old woman on a bicycle, and a flock of ducks. With the exception of the ducks, no one was wearing native costume.

We took a few pictures of the tiny houses and caught the 4:50 ferry home.

When we left Ribe on Thursday morning, there were only three more days of travel ahead of us. The realization that an experience was coming to an end which could never be repeated in just the same way made us sad.

As usual, we were late getting started. It seems incredible that after more than seven weeks together, we were still unable to calculate the time necessary for dressing, eating breakfast, paying the bill, loading the car, and getting started at a given hour—but it was none the less so.

To make this phenomenon even more puzzling, we were almost always exactly thirty-five minutes behind our starting schedule—we seldom varied more than a minute or two either way, although the cause of the delay was always different.

One would have thought that after a time we would have become accustomed to being thirty-five minutes late and taken the matter in our stride—perhaps even figured on it—but we never did. As a result, there was always a certain amount of surprised hysteria in the air by the time we reached the bill-paying stage.

On this particular morning, our non-English-speaking porter spent a maddeningly long time sorting the usual bits of paper and deducing from them how much we owed. When he finally presented us with the bill, we handed him in payment our Ribehus coupons taken from the coupon book which we had bought and paid for in Bennett's Oslo travel office weeks before.

Had we handed him a hat check from the Grand Hotel in Shanghai, he could not have been less receptive. Obviously he had never heard of Mr. Bennett or his coupons, and it is a complicated system to explain to anyone when both parties are confined to throwing their arms about.

After fifteen minutes of this it became evident that the porter was in better physical condition than we were and that, unless we changed the debating rules, he would eventually win. So George and I broke contact and went to the Ribe Tourist Association, leaving Sara and Lucy to sit on the luggage and glare.

It must have been a terrible ordeal for the porter, for when we returned with the obliging young man from the Bureau, the poor fellow was clinging to the edge of the desk, bathed in sweat. There followed a half hour's debate in Danish which ended in complete victory for our side. We wrung the young man's hand, threw contemptuous glances at the unfortunate porter and headed north for Aarhus, an hour behind schedule.

It was a singing day, the air crisp with the first touch of fall. The road from Ribe to Aarhus wanders in a northeasterly direction through the most beautiful section of Jutland. It is a rolling, carefully tended country of great farms surrounding groups of white, thatch-roofed farm buildings, a country of ducks and geese and cows and chickens, obese pigs and rotund work horses—a country of contented abundance, its hands folded across its stomach.

Three great, tan horses came over the horizon pulling a plow behind them, a colt striding along manfully beside its mother, and the cameras came out of their cases as one. We photographed our way to Jelling, stalking flocks of geese, big-barreled horses, slowly turning windmills, and redcoated postmen. We took pictures with that pleasant abandon which comes to all photographers at the end of a long trip when they find rolls and rolls of unused film at the bottom of the camera bag.

Jelling, pronounced Yelling, contains the great burial mounds of King Gorm the Old, the first king of all Denmark, who ruled during the early part of the tenth century with his queen, known according to Sydney Clark as Thyra the Beautiful. Beside each mound is a runic stone and between them the nine-hundred-year-old village church crouches timidly like a setting hen.

What really intrigued us, however, was the fact that Gorm and Thyra the Beautiful were the parents of our friend Harold Bluetooth. To a woman like Thyra who, judging by her name, must have put some stress on personal appearance, it must have been a trial to have a son who was to carry a name like Harold's through the pages of history.

The runic stone beside Gorm's funeral mound was set up by Harold who states, with becoming modesty: "Harold, the King, had this stone raised to Gorm his father and Thyra his mother— *the* Harold who conquered the whole of Denmark and Norway and made the Danes Christian."

We continued northward leaving Jelling behind. In a town near Silkeborg we bought bread, cheese and milk, which we ate sitting on a grassy bank beside a country road looking out across a stubble field from which the wheat had been recently cut. It was a pleasant meal, although overshadowed by the knowledge that it was almost the last of a long succession of similar lunches eaten by lakes and glacial streams, in the aqueous, green light of forests, in fertile valleys and on snow-blanketed highlands.

It was going to take quite a while to get this sort of thing out of our systems.

2 3

North Jutland

AT SILKEBORG THE ORTHODOX TRAVELER IS EXPECTED TO take a boat trip through a chain of lakes. The travel books are very firm on this point.

There was a cold wind blowing down the lovely, tree-shaded river through which the sight-seeing steamers pass on the first leg of their journey. It was much more comfortable in the car than it would be on the deck of any steamer, but no one dared mention this obvious fact.

A boat trip was about the last thing we would have chosen at that moment, but it was down in the books as a triple "must," and once a person becomes a traveler with a capital T his attitude toward such things undergoes a curious change. As a resident of New York I have never taken a guided tour through Radio City or climbed the Statue of Liberty. I doubt if I will ever take a boat trip around Manhattan Island. I even know a man in Buffalo who takes pride in the fact that he has never seen Niagara Falls. I am sure, however, that if I were a Scandinavian, visiting the United States as a Tourist, I would do all of these things eagerly and, if possible, on the first day.

Sara sneezed and pawed around in her bag for a paper handkerchief. Lucy looked hopeful.

"You really *are* getting a cold," she said.

"Maybe I can stay below and look through a porthole," said Sara, dabbing at her nose.

"Is this really a good trip?" asked Lucy, who always acted as if George and I had been born and brought up in whatever locality we happened to be in.

We reminded her that we were strangers here ourselves and read to her the passage, describing the beauties of the boat trip. Lucy sighed.

George got out and went down a flight of steps to the steamer office. He returned beaming.

"We've just missed a boat," he said. "There won't be another for an hour."

We agreed that there was nothing to do but wait.

Sara sneezed again. A cold blast of wind shook the car.

"It seems like a terrible thing to do," said George, "but maybe we had better skip the trip on account of Sara."

A look of guilty relief came into everyone's face.

"I hate to spoil the fun," said Sara, playing the thing through to the end.

George and I turned the car over to Lucy and slept soundly in the back seat until we reached Aarhus.

Aarhus is a big city port on the east coast of Jutland, but like most Danish cities, it doesn't sacrifice charm to size. If it had contained nothing but the Hotel Royal, we would have been satisfied.

The Royal is built in the grand old manner of a grand old era. One could march troops ten abreast up its main staircase. In New York our bedrooms would have been cut up into four-room apartments, and one could put on a cocktail party in any of the bathrooms. The plumbing was in scale, with wash basins big as card tables, eight-foot bathtubs, and huge fixtures of gleaming brass.

Lucy and Sara were so fascinated by this prodigal luxury that they could not have been lured away from it if the Vale of Kashmir had been right around the corner. So, George and I went sightseeing by ourselves.

The Number One attraction in Aarhus is *Den Gamly By* or, to make it simpler, "The Old Town." Here, in the midst of a park, the Danes have reconstructed an ancient village complete with inn, mill, storehouses, shops and dwellings, all transported from their original sites and reassembled beam by beam and brick by brick with the antiquarian zeal which lurks in the breast of all Scandinavians.

The Danish Travel Bureau produces some beautiful colored posters. One of the most alluring portrays a millpond surrounded by old buildings, their pink half-timbers and weathered bricks merging with the soft gray-green of weeping willows. Out of the black shadows cast by the overhanging foliage a family of ducks is paddling into the sunlight.

That was the scene that had originally sold George and me on Denmark. No one had ever been able to tell us just where it was located, although we had made many inquiries, for it was the kind of place that one dreamed about when faced with the need for a few days of rest with a good book. Then, in *Den Gamly By*, we rounded the corner of an old yellow building and there it was. Even the family of ducks was just emerging from the shadows. We had found our oasis in the middle of an outdoor museum in the middle of a city.

Friday, September 1, was Lucy's birthday. A huge box of birthday candy from an immaculate little shop in the shadow of the cathedral caused both Lucy and Sara to set out for *Den Gamly By* in high spirits.

On the previous afternoon, all the ancient little houses had been shut and George and I had had to satisfy our curiosity by flattening our noses against the windows of the bakery, the hatmaker's, the watchmaker's, and the village bindery. Now, however, the town was open for business and what was more, it was out to get it.

A short man in a sports jacket and a derby pounced on us as we were passing the old tavern and dragged us inside together with a young Danish couple whom he had scooped up at the same time. He then locked the door, which made us rather nervous, and began to lecture rapidly in Danish, which made us more so.

He took us through every room in the tavern without interrupting his flow of words and then, still talking, led us across the street to the watchmaker's where he locked us in again for another lecture. Eventually he began to show signs of exhaustion and turned us over to a large, forbidding-looking woman with a black mustache who was standing by as his relief. She locked us successively in the bakery and the bindery, making only one concession to the English language. Each time she finished with a room she turned to us and said: "Let's go."

Once, we took her at her word and sneaked down the hall when her back was turned. We did not have time to unlock the big front door, however, before she caught us and shooed us back, angrily. After that we relaxed.

As an antidote to the very old, Aarhus offers, as its Number Two attraction, an ultramodern Town Hall. The Scandinavians have a passion for Town Halls and lavish as much loving care and money on them as Americans do on their stadiums and railroad stations. The first thing a citizen of Oslo asks is whether you have seen the Town Hall. The Stockholm Town Hall is world famous. Copenhagen has so many public buildings that we were never quite sure which was the Town Hall, but we understood that it was terrific. Aarhus tried to side-step competition by going so modern that it will take years for the world to catch up with it.

Somewhat exhausted by it all, we lunched at the Royal on the longest omelet in the world. Danish omelets can only be referred to on a footage basis. This one must have had a full thirty-six-inch spread from tip to tip. We coped with it to the best of our limited ability and then parted from this fascinating city with regret, planning to have a quick look at the University of Aarhus on our way out to Hvidsten Kro.

It is hard to tell why Sydney Clark's description of the Great Hall of the University of Aarhus intrigued us as it did. He had merely said that after being almost destroyed during World War II, it was restored in 1946 and that "its light woodwork is enhanced by several novelties including strange, spiral light fixtures and a circle of wall benches upholstered in black and white calfskin."

I am quite sure that most of us had seen spiral light fixtures many times without giving them too much attention, and anyone who has ever been to El Morocco in New York has a good working idea of what black and white calfskin looks like. In spite of this we all seemed to feel that, having come so far, it would be a shame not to have a look at these wonders of the Great Hall.

After an hour of diligent searching, during which nobody either spoke English or knew where the Great Hall was, or both, we located a building which, by a process of elimination, we decided must be the one we were seeking. Two sad-faced youths, who looked to us like students, were sitting on a low wall near the entrance. When we asked them if the building behind them contained spiral light fixtures and black and white calfskin seats, they shook their heads mournfully. "This is our first day," they said.

We were becoming frustrated. The search for the Great Hall was threatening to throw our time schedule out of gear for the rest of the trip, but for the sake of general morale we could not let go now. I entered the building and found what might very well be the Bursar's office. There the work of the university was humming along with the quiet efficiency which one would expect to find in such a place. A young woman with spectacles left her desk to find out what the strange-looking man wanted.

"Excuse me," I said in slow and precise English, "is there a room—or Great Hall—connected with the building, containing spiral light fixtures and a circular wall bench in black and white calfskin?"

Her eyes reflected alarm, but her voice was composed. "This is the Rector's office," she said with dignity.

"I know," I explained, "but we wish to see the spiral lighting fixtures and the black and white——"

She was backing away from me now. "Black and white?" she said. "I do not understand. I will get the Rector."

"No, no," I protested in a panic, "it doesn't really matter. We were just passing by and we wanted to see the spiral——"

It was beginning all over again. I fled through the ultramodern glass doors to the street. During my brief absence Sara and Lucy had captured a little Danish boy on a bicycle and were carrying on some research of their own.

The boy was jabbering in an unintelligible mixture of Danish and English to which Lucy and Sara were listening with the concentrated attention of people who cannot understand a word. He stopped suddenly. "I will ride ahead," he said.

He then threw himself on his bicycle and rode madly down the street. We followed him as he wound his way up one side street and down another. "He said he would ride ahead," remarked George finally, "but he didn't say where to."

The little boy took a turn to the right toward the city. "To hell with it," said Sara. She turned left and headed north to Hvidsten Kro.

In Danish Kro means inn and Hvidsten is the name of a small farm center several miles north of Aarhus. We were going there because Mogens Lichtenberg wanted us to spend at least one night in a typical Danish country inn and had told us a story about this one which made us eager to meet the people who ran it.

In 1943, he said, when the resistance movement in Denmark was just beginning, the British had established contact with the owner of Hvidsten Kro, one Marius Fiil, who organized what became known as the Hvidsten Group. This consisted of his son Niels, his son-in-law Peder Sørensen and five young men from the village. His wife and three daughters were also active.

Each night British planes dropped war materials to this group. These were hidden and eventually distributed. This went on for almost a year, but in March, 1944, the Aarhus Gestapo caught up with the situation and the wife of Marius Fiil saw her husband, her son, two of her daughters and her son-in-law led away to death or worse. Her parting words to them were, "Don't fear. You did nothing wrong."

Three months later the eight men of the Hvidsten Group were shot. Two of the Fiils' daughters were sent to German prisons where they remained until after the war. Today, the mother and the three daughters carry on the inn and at a road intersection nearby a great boulder bears the names of the men who died rather than recognize defeat.

We found the inn with some difficulty, hidden away in a network of narrow country roads. It was a long, low building with a heavily thatched roof, the rough edges of which provided an admirable means of putting out a traveler's eyes on dark nights. A good-looking girl in slacks and bone glasses, whom we rightly guessed to be one of the Fiils' daughters, showed us to our rooms in an immaculate little guest house in the rear.

Inside, the inn was cut up into numerous rooms opening one into another and all filled with country people eating and drinking. We arranged for a private dining room and then strolled down the road, past the boulder monument and through the little village. A huge Percheron was being shod in a blacksmith shop so small that three-quarters of the animal's tan bulk stuck out into the road. A bakery, built to the same scale, was belching black smoke and throwing off the sweet smell of fresh bread. A flock of young geese waddled self-importantly across the road. In the fields on either side were fat, red cows and along the fence beside us, four young calves galloped frantically toward a watering trough.

It was a static, bounteous world in which time played only a minor part. At that moment the road wound around the foot of a steep hill and we were face to face with an enormous oil derrick. On the side of the tool house beside it was a sign: "Danish-American Exploration Company—Gulf Oil."

The caretaker came out to greet us. This was American equipment and he was proud of it. The hole was down sixty-nine hundred feet and was going to twelve thousand. Then if nothing happened they proposed to give it up. The caretaker was so pleased with the enormity of the figures that it was obviously of secondary (if any) importance to him whether a drop of oil was ever brought to the surface. It was the hole that counted with him rather than its contents.

We went back to the Inn to discuss this phenomenon with anyone we could find. No one seemed to be particularly interested.

"But don't you want them to strike oil?"

"Why should we?"

"Because all the land around here will then become very valuable and everyone will be rich."

"Ah, yes, but it will spoil our land. This is a beautiful place. If they put oil derricks all over it, it will no longer be a place to live."

Lucy's birthday party was staged in a room with blue-green panels trimmed with red. The walls were covered with copper and brass utensils. A wood-burning stove stood in one corner and in the other, a brown and green grandfather clock. There were Danish and American flags on the table, flanking a great bowl of wild roses.

We were told, somewhat apologetically, that there was only one dinner at the Hvidsten Kro which never varied. They hoped we would like it. It was a memorable meal, its successive courses borne in to us on platters as big as serving trays.

For the first course we had herring (pickled), beef, cheese, bread and butter and *snaps*.

For the second course we had scrambled eggs with pork.

For the third course we had beef tongue (cold), served with carrots, cabbage and leeks.

For the fourth course we had pork sausage, fried potatoes, and wonderful pickled red cabbage sitting in a huge sausage ring.

For the fifth course we had sausage cakes, cucumber, bologna, preserved apples, mustard pickles, liverwurst, and cold fried fish.

By the time we had finished the fifth course and washed all five down with two bottles of wine, we were reasonably close to paralysis.

At this point, the food suddenly stopped coming in. That was all right with us, but we did not want to hurt anyone's feelings by leaving the table when possibly they were preparing some Gargantuan dessert.

I finally rose with some difficulty and opened the door into the kitchen. Mrs. Fiil and her daughters were working there with several helpers. "Is there anything else coming?" I asked.

Those who understood my question looked up with astonishment, mixed with admiration. One could see that in the back of their minds was the thought that here, perhaps, they had met their master. "Do you want anything else?" asked the pretty Fiils' daughter with the bone glasses, who was the spokesman for the family when it came to English.

"Good God, no," I said and closed the door quietly, leaving them somewhat puzzled.

This extraordinary meal cost us seventy-five cents each, excluding the *snaps* and the wine and the after-dinner coffee. Those three items cost each of us a dollar seventy-five. Clearly, in Denmark, it is more economical to die from thirst than from starvation.

We helped each other down the lane to the guest house. Lucy had had her birthday party.

We breakfasted next morning in the blue-green dining room. The sun was streaming through the windows and it did not seem possible that tragedy in military boots could have pounded across these scrubbed floor boards such a short time before.

Mrs. Fiil and her three daughters came in while we were eating. They had heard that we knew the story and that we were interested. Mrs. Fiil said something in Danish and one of the girls brought a bottle which she described as "Morning Bitters." We drank to Denmark and to the people who had died for it, and they drank to the United States and their gratitude for the help which had been given them through ECA.

This was our last day of travel—the last day that we were to put our luggage into the back end of the Plymouth and set forth for unknown places. We were to spend it well off the beaten path, traveling north on secondary roads on our way to Aalborg where the night boat would take us back to Copenhagen.

A few miles north of Hvidsten Kro we came on the charming village of Mariager. It gave us a feeling of accomplishment to find that Sydney Clark and Clara Laughlin were silent about this dream village hidden away at the end of a North Jutland fjord. At last we had turned up something for ourselves.

It was a tiny place with narrow cobbled streets and half-timbered cottages. In the center of the village, in a little square, a bronze statue poured a stream of water into a public watering trough. And everywhere were roses—they covered the walls of gardens, climbed across the sides of houses and over the edges of the steeply sloping roofs.

Just before entering the village we had made another discovery in the form of an old church and cloister which deserves more attention than it gets from the Tourist Bureaus. It must be at least six centuries old and appears to have been torn down, rebuilt, and pushed around in the manner of all Scandinavian churches through the centuries.

We were shown through it by a Danish guide. When we tried to explain that we were Americans and did not understand a word that he was saying he looked at us with hurt astonishment, apparently resenting interruption, particularly in a foreign language that *he* did not understand. He then continued his story in voluble Danish to the bitter end after which he bowed, accepted our tip and led us to the door, as one satisfied with a job well done.

On our way out we met a young man with a brief case hurrying along a graveled path beneath the trees. We asked him a question about the church to which he replied in Oxford English and immediately offered to show it to us. So we saw it all over again—in English.

He was a friendly chap, and after he had explained the church he took us to the cloister which stands directly behind it and is now used as the office of the local judge. Behind the cloister were the fish ponds where the holy men of old spent their leisure time angling for cod. It didn't seem to be just the place where one would have expected to catch cod, but that was what the judge told us.

In Mariager we bought the usual cheese, marmalade, milk, bread and butter and drove to Hahoe to eat our lunch.

Just what Hahoe is (or was) we will perhaps never know, for Sydney and Clara are silent on this point also. It was, therefore, our third discovery. Our friend at Mariager had told us to go there for lunch and enjoy the view, but he had not bothered us with historical background. We were not even sure of the name.

Two great mounds sit on the top of what is, for Denmark, a high hill. A circular path spirals to the top of the biggest mound. From there one can look out for miles across Jutland, over rolling farmland, lakes, and stands of timber. Below us was Mariager and the fjord, reflecting the white clouds and the deep blue of the sky.

It was our last picnic. At the bottom of the hill, where we joined the main road again, we met three little boys pushing bicycles laboriously up the grade. Sara and Lucy decided that they were just the ones to receive the remaining contents of the picnic basket. So we stopped them and delivered into their astonished hands half a dozen kinds of cheese, half-finished jars of marmalade and jam and, what was to them the most impressive of all, handfuls of chocolates. This last was a generous impulse of Lucy's which did not sit well with the rest of us, as it was the expensive birthday present which we had bought for her the day before in Aarhus.

Everyone who talked to us about North Jutland had insisted that we stop at Rebild. This is a park set aside as a Danish-American shrine, and here each year the Fourth of July is celebrated with what appears to be more reverence and respect than is accorded the festival by its celebrants in the United States. Three or four thousand Danish-Americans attend these meetings and it is said that the crowds run to forty or fifty thousand in all.

It was an elusive place, situated in a forest and off the main road. When we finally located it, a beautiful Danish girl offered to guide us to what she referred to as the Log Cabin. We had no idea what that was, but she was the kind of a girl that one follows without hesitation.

It turned out to be a Gargantuan cabin built of enormous logs which, she told us, were contributed by each state in the United States. On the hill above it the Stars and Stripes whipped in the wind beside the Danish flag. She unlocked the door and departed. A man appeared from nowhere and sold us four tickets, which he immediately took back again for future use. We were left to our own resources.

Facing us were a Conestoga wagon, a burnt-wood picture of Lincoln, a life-size model of an Indian chief in full regalia, a large piece of California redwood, several prints of Niagara Falls, an ox yoke and various other bits of Americana.

The ticket man who had made himself comfortable on the door-step seemed to be upset by the speed with which we covered the exhibit. There was nothing disrespectful in our attitude, however, for there should be a Rebild in every country—perhaps many of them. We were merely experts in such matters.

Mogens Lichtenberg had told us about the Tingbaek mine which was on our road to Aalborg. It is an old abandoned limestone and chalk mine which was used by the Danish sculptor Bundgaard as his workshop and studio when he was unable to find any other place large enough for his great pieces, such as the Gefion Fountain in Copenhagen.

We found an old farmer near the entrance puttering around in a pair of wooden shoes who seemed to be the caretaker. At any rate, he turned and entered the mine as soon as he saw us and we followed him. Here, in the huge, damp, vaulted chambers that had been hewn out of the limestone, Bundgaard had worked alone. His original models are still there, full-size, illuminated by the bleak rays from hundred-watt electric-light bulbs. On the limestone walls, the sculptor had amused himself in his off moments by carving bas-reliefs. Dark mysterious passages led off in all directions. It was not a place that we would have chosen for our atelier.

In spite of all our sight-seeing it was only two o'clock in the afternoon when we reached Aalborg, so we kept right on to Blokhus and the great beaches of the northwest coast.

These Danish beaches put our American counterparts to shame. They are a half mile wide, flat and hard as a table top and because there appears to be little rise and fall of tide along these shores they are remarkably free from litter.

The little summer village of Blokhus was closed and boarded up for the season. We put the car on the sand, pushed the speedometer needle up to the sixty mark and drove mile after mile northward toward a thin yellow line of cliffs which never seemed to come any nearer.

The blue sky of morning had been replaced by a heavy overcast and a strong, cold wind was blowing in from the northwest. We were all alone on those endless sands except for a few sea gulls which followed us because there was not anything more promising in sight. It was only necessary to move the wheel an inch or two from time to time to avoid a piece of driftwood. It became monotonous. We turned around and retraced our course. At the place where we had come onto the beach, some brave Danes were trying the bathing, which from casual observation they found rather grim.

We hated to leave that beach. At Aalborg we would have dinner and then take the night boat for Copenhagen. From that moment, we would be more or less on our way home. The beach at Blokhus was Journey's End. We stopped the car and got out.

To the amazement of the bathing Danes who had come to the water's edge to shiver and watch, George, who seldom gives way to emotional expression or symbolic rhythm, suddenly began a slow, circular tribal dance. Without a word, Sara fell in behind him, then Lucy, then I. George became visibly excited, leaping into the air, running in great circles and flinging his arms toward the lowering clouds. We followed him as best we could, knowing that George was saying farewell to Scandinavia. The Danes, who did not share this knowledge, conversed together in low tones, then moved out into deeper water, ignoring the cold.

We dined at the Kilden Restaurant on the outskirts of the city. Outside it had begun to rain and the big drops, splashing against the plate-glass windows, fitted into our mood.

Unflagging to the last in our efforts to obtain from the Norwegians, the Swedes, or the Danes, those articles of food and drink which were peculiarly indigenous to the United States, we ordered Martinis. Did they understand the Martini? The sleek headwaiter gave the impression of understanding it far better than we did. Did he know just how Americans liked their Martinis mixed? Perhaps the ladies and gentlemen would care to state the features that pleased them most in Martinis. This led us to the suspicion that he was a big bluff who did not have the foggiest notion about them, but we explained in detail and in words of one syllable—four parts American gin, one part of dry French vermouth, a twist of lemon peel and serve.

The headwaiter listened patiently and respectfully. He was so intelligent in his listening that we changed the order to double Martinis. When they arrived he had carried out our directions to the letter. Four parts gin, one part vermouth—untouched and undiluted, however, by ice. We gave up and sipped these tepid depth charges moodily while the world about us rocked itself to bits.

We were no longer despondent. Why worry about the trip being over? There was nothing to prevent us starting again in Norway and going around the second time. We ordered the best of wines and drank toasts to the honor of Scandinavia and the United States.

At this particular moment, the hand of Fate caused the Danish-American Club of Aalborg to file solemnly into the dining room of the Kilden and seat itself at a long table immediately beside us. As soon as we discovered the nature of this rather morose-looking group, we naturally considered ourselves God's gift to Danish-

American societies and immediately entered into negotiations with the group leader.

He was a worried-looking man who told us that the club met periodically and that this was one of the periodic meetings. Other than that there seemed little for him to say about the society. We did our best to keep the conversation animated without any great success and finally finished off our excellent wine with several brief, but impassioned speeches on the relations between Denmark and the United States. It was our public farewell to Scandinavia.

It was an hour before the sailing time of the supermodern marine palace that was to take us to Copenhagen. We drove the car aboard and went on the town afoot. As might have been expected on this extraordinary day, we immediately ran into a street fair, where we poured out our remaining kroner like water. Later that night as we lay in our bunks, the blare of the music, the confusion of the whirling lights and the voices of the pushing crowds, blended in our sleepy brains into Scandinavia's farewell to us.

WHERE END MEETS BEGINNING

O.S.P.

Where End Meets Beginning

AT FIVE-THIRTY MONDAY AFTERNOON AN EXTRAORDINARILY
polite young man called at the d'Angleterre to drive us, in our own
car, to the Copenhagen airport. There he left us in front of the
main building after many deep bows had been exchanged.

We watched the Plymouth fade out of sight in the dusk as one
would watch his child being led away by a stranger. It had been
our home for fifty-four days. It had taken us through the fjords and
the ice fields of Norway, through the forests and wheatlands of
Sweden, through the bicycles and over the beaches of Denmark,
all without hitch or mishap. Now, left standing outside the Copenhagen airport building beside a pile of rather battered suitcases,
we felt suddenly helpless and abandoned.

The plane door was closed. The big motors were warming up. We
were moving down the runway to our take-off position. Then we
were in the air and, through the smoky, half-darkness the lights of
Copenhagen swung into view over the wing tip as we banked to
the right.

An indescribably sharp depression closed over us. It was like being
torn from a loved one. We wanted to cry out against this outrage,
but we knew it was useless. We were chips in a stream—chips
which had momentarily circled in a lovely eddy and were now

being swept back into the main current. The roaring of the motors outside the windows symbolized our helplessness.

Headwinds in the mid-Atlantic drove us north to Iceland. It was a broken night and then, just about the time that the sleeping pills were beginning to work, we were awakened by the voice of the captain coming over the loud-speaker. He wished us good morning. We were off the southern coast of Greenland. The captain thought we might be interested to see it. The captain thanked us and lapsed into silence.

Heaven knew what time it was. It was dawn. That was all we knew. The kind of time that primitive man went by.

But even dawn had taken on a new aspect. All night long, while we slept, we had been skimming over the surface of a world that was turning ponderously toward the sun—skimming westward through the earth's thin envelope of air like a swimmer struggling desperately to escape a pursuer.

It had been a losing race, for now the sun was at our heels and bearing down on us fast. We were flying low. Two miles to our right lay a savage coast line—barren mountains, covered with snow and ice, rising vertically from a slate-gray sea—the light-green ice of glaciers creeping through the high mountain valleys to their ultimate destruction in the ocean—the line of darker green at their edges where huge pieces had broken off and fallen into the water below.

Two deep fjords carved and twisted their way inland through the mountains, black night still lingering in their depths. In the ocean below us, icebergs and fields of broken ice floated, motionless. To the west a deep band of indigo-blue ran across the horizon, topped by another of rose.

On our right the rounded cowlings of our starboard engines, haloed by the transparent glint of their whirling propellers, were outlined against the rocky chaos. It was a striking contrast—those savagely lonely mountains, spewing ice into the freezing water below as they had been spewing it for aeons, forming the background for these delicate, immensely complicated bits of machinery.

This world we gazed down upon was beautiful, but it was the beauty of a tiger seen from a vantage point of safety. What lay below would tear and destroy whatever came into its clutches as ruthlessly as ever a tiger clawed its prey.

Our particular vantage point of safety was created by those four glittering halos which began to sparkle more and more brightly as the day caught up with us. The machines which created the halos were a composite of thousands of parts, each one of which must perform a complex and essential function at a given instant of time or all the other parts must cease to perform.

This fantastic series of co-ordinations was taking place many times each minute. Should one part fail, then gradually the shiny halos would grow dim and the outlines of the whirling propellers would emerge, turning more and more slowly and finally stopping, transformed from Power to curiously shaped and utterly useless bits of steel.

That this intricate sequence could go on uninterrupted hour after hour, was nothing short of a miracle. Surely the odds must be a billion to one against it, yet inside the body of the plane the passengers dozed in a state of complete relaxation, looking down occasionally at the back of the tiger with bored, disinterested eyes.

Did the passengers represent perhaps Faith—old-fashioned Faith in a new-fashioned cellophane package—Faith in man and in his eventual destiny—a faith which has enabled him to conquer continents with his bare hands, and to move across the surface of the earth at will—a faith which has enabled him to conquer material obstacles, which has put him on the verge of conquering time and space and which may ultimately enable him to make the greatest conquest of all—himself?

It was all getting fuzzy at the edges and in another moment I would have been asleep. "You know," said George, breaking a long silence, "the whole thing reminds me of an experience I had many years ago in the Canadian Rockies. Of course, it was long before the Banff-Jasper highway had been even dreamed of. There was a man by the name of Job Walters——"

"Would you care for any orange or tomato juice?" asked the hostess. God knows where she had spent the night. She looked as if it had been in the most restful and comfortable of beds. The heads of Lucy and Sara appeared suddenly over the tops of the seats in front of us.

"Did you say orange juice?" asked Lucy.

"Fresh orange juice?" added Sara cautiously.

"Of course," said the hostess.

"Not buttered toast?" said Sara incredulously.

"Oh yes," said the hostess.

Lucy and Sara looked at each other.

"I think I'll go and tidy my hair," said Lucy.

Behind us the coast of Greenland began to drop below the horizon and a soft blanket of clouds was drawn under the plane.

In a few hours the little foursome which had been living together so closely and so harmoniously for almost eight weeks would have disintegrated and its components would already be rolling in old, accustomed grooves.

Lucy, surrounded by travel-stained clothes, would be glued to the telephone, re-establishing the lines to children and grandchildren. Miles out in the country Sara would be doing the same. George in his studio would be scratching his head not knowing just where to start or if he even wanted to.

I would have shaken hands with everyone in the office, told them all what a wonderful time we had had and faced up to a great pile of accumulated (and for the most part unimportant) papers. The telephone would be ringing and a man with a beaming face would be approaching my desk whose name, for the moment, I could not recall.

Memorandum
to Travelers

WE SPENT FIFTY-THREE DAYS IN SCANDINAVIA, STARTING with Oslo and ending with Copenhagen. During that time we motored thirty-seven hundred miles through Norway, Sweden and Denmark—not much by United States standards, but a lot in those countries.

It was much too short a time but seventy-five days or a hundred days would have been equally inadequate, for given more time we would have tried to go to more places. The answer to "How much time is enough?" is, "How much time have you got?" My only suggestion is that no one try to take the same trip in *less* than fifty-three days if he has any tendency to dizziness.

Because our stay was so short we were forced to leave out many places that we wanted to see and, because we knew nothing whatever about the three countries, we went to a few places that we would undoubtedly skip on a second round. These we have indicated below, but there is extraordinarily little that we would change.

From the point of view of dramatic climax, perhaps our route should have been reversed, starting with little Denmark, going north through Sweden and ending on the crashing Wagnerian chords of Norway. To have done that it would have been necessary to start the trip in the middle of June, however, and we were limited by circumstances to the period from July 13 to September 4.

Norwegian weather sets the schedule. On the west coast it is nothing to write travel folders about at best and as far as we could make out, its best, from a motorist's point of view, is compressed into six weeks from June 15 to August 1.

We spent eighteen days in Norway. From Oslo we motored to the west coast, then north through the fjord country to Trondheim. At Trondheim we turned east into Sweden making a beeline across country to the Gulf of Bothnia at Sundsval, from which point we ricocheted south after the manner of a pinball for twenty days and eventually crossed into Denmark at Hälsingborg. We were in Denmark fifteen days. After a week in Copenhagen we made a circuit of the country districts, taking a night boat back to Copenhagen from North Jutland, and flying home from there.

I am reproducing our itinerary, not because it represents the ideal or the only trip, but because it was developed with "blood, sweat and tears" and may serve as a starting point for someone else to build a better one.

The hotels mentioned were not always the hotels at which we stayed. They are the hotels which struck us as the best, however. That does not mean that there are not others which are excellent. Hotel standards in all three countries are amazingly high.

Everyone is so eager to be helpful that planning a Scandinavian trip should be easy. However, the very enthusiasm of the Norwegians, Swedes and Danes for their own countries can be a stumbling block. Put a map in front of any one of them and his eyes will grow dreamy. Then he will probably begin drawing circles on the map with his forefinger and say "Ah, this is a wonderful region. You must see everything here. And down here—ah, beautiful. You must spend a lot of time there." Such conferences usually end up with the over-all conclusion that you should see everything.

Finally, with the help of half a dozen itineraries prepared with

225

the aid of interested nationals and a few books on Scandinavia written in England and the United States, we came up with something that at least fitted into the available time. Just when all seemed set we discovered that one of the "musts" in Sweden is a visit to Rättvik on Sunday when the inhabitants of the region put on their native costumes and go to church.

Obviously that was something that could not be missed, although under cross-examination it would have been hard to tell just why. It should not be too difficult, however, to arrive somewhere on Sunday. Rättvik was on the itinerary, but unfortunately our arrival there happened to fall on Tuesday. After two weeks of reading and consultation the schedule was pushed around so that Rättvik fell into place on the right day, but from that time on it became a thorn in the side. No matter what we wanted to do, we were blocked by the necessity of being in Rättvik on Sunday.

At last the itinerary was complete and typed. At that moment we were asked to a cocktail party to meet a famous Scandinavian. The first thing he wanted to see was our itinerary. As we watched his face it was obvious that this was the most insane schedule he had ever looked at. He asked if he might keep it for a day or two in order to give the matter careful thought. We appreciated this, of course, but silently hoped that it would not be longer, for we were already late in reserving our hotel accommodations.

Days went by. At the end of a week we phoned him. He said that what bothered him was that we were not spending enough time in the cities. We explained that if we spent more time in the cities we would have to spend less in the country. He said that of course was out of the question, but couldn't we take a few extra weeks? We said we could not. Couldn't we then omit one or both of the countries of which he was not a national? When he found we could not, he hoped we would have a wonderful time. Another week wasted.

Then we met a second Scandinavian at a party given to bring us together. We should have refused all such invitations or locked the itinerary in the office safe marked "Top Secret." Of course we were going to Lapland and the North Cape? We immediately put our new adviser on notice that we could not take an extra three or four weeks. He became excited. The North Cape country was the most interesting part of Scandinavia, in his opinion. In fact he gave us the feeling that for his money we could put the rest of the trip in our hats. Fly to Tromsö! Live with the Lapps! Fly back! Cut out the south if necessary, but go north without fail!

After several sleepless nights we lunched with a third Scandinavian. He had two reasons for advising against the North Cape. One, there was nothing to see when you got there, and two, you probably wouldn't see it anyway on account of the fog. Another week gone.

The Göta Canal meanders southwestward from Stockholm to Göteborg. One may go through it by boat in three days. We had decided against it until I met an enthusiastic Swede at luncheon. He was horrified at our decision to omit it. "The Göta trip," he said, "is one of the most beautiful and unique in Europe. I beg you, sir— on my bended knees I beg you—do not miss it."

Rather than have him go to all that trouble in a public place, we changed our itinerary and made arrangements to have the car driven from Stockholm to Göteborg by a young man from the Royal Swedish Automobile Club. We were then asked to meet a highly intelligent Swedish lady at dinner.

"The Göta Canal!" she exclaimed and there was genuine horror in her voice. "Three days in that *ditch*, jammed into a little canal boat with God knows who. I hope you hit a three-day rainstorm." We had not thought of that. Arrangements were canceled and we resumed our schedule as originally planned and made a solemn pact not to mention our itinerary to anyone else until we were on the plane.

Here is the itinerary.

JULY

Thurs. 13 Leave Idlewild Airport, New York (Scandinavian Airlines System)   11:30 A.M.
                 Arrive Gander, Newfoundland 5:10 P.M.
(Fri.   14)   "   Prestwick, Scotland   5:05 A.M.
                  "   Oslo, Norway   9:35 A.M.

NORWAY

			Approximate miles
Fri.	14	Oslo (Grand Hotel—front rooms—or Bristol)	
Sat.	15	"	
Sun.	16	Geilo via Honefoss and Gol (Holms Høyfjellshotel)	155
Mon.	17	Lofthus via Haugastöl and Fossli (Hotel Ullensvang)	80
Tues.	18	"	
Wed.	19	Bergen. Ferry from Kinsarvik to Kvanndal (Hotel Norge)	95
Thurs.	20	"	
Fri.	21	Stalheim via Eide and Vossevangen (Stalheim Turisthotel)	137
Sat.	22	Balestrand. Ferry from Gudvangen to Balholm (Kvikne Hotel)	*Mostly ferry*
Sun.	23	"	
Mon.	24	Loen via Mjeld and Utvik (Alexandra Hotel)	95
Tues.	25	"	
Wed.	26	Geiranger via Grotli (Union Hotel)	77
Thurs.	27	"	
Fri.	28	Åndalsnes via ferry to Sylte (Grand Hotel Bellevue)	70
Sat.	29	Dombås (Dombås Turisthotel)	120
Sun.	30	Trondheim via Opdal and Stören (Hotel Britannia)	140
Mon.	31	"	

SWEDEN

AUGUST

Tues.	1	Åre via Verdalsöyra (Åregården Hotel)	130
Wed.	2	Sundsvall via Östersund and the Indalsälven (Hotel Knaust)	190
Thurs.	3	Gävle via Söderhamn (Grand Central Hotel)	115

Fri.	4	Rättvik via Falun (Hotel Siljansborg)	121
Sat.	5	"	
Sun.	6	"	
Mon.	7	Uppsala via Leksand and Enköping (Hotel Gillet)	80
Tues.	8	Stockholm (Grand Hotel or Hotel Stockholm)	40
Wed.	9	"	
Thurs.	10	"	
Fri.	11	"	
Sat.	12	"	
Sun.	13	"	
Mon.	14	"	
Tues.	15	"	
Wed.	16	Gränna via Norrköping and Linköping (Gyllene Uttern)	190
Thurs.	17	Göteborg via Jönköping and Borås (Park Avenue Hotel)	120
Fri.	18	"	
Sat.	19	Båstad via Varberg (Skånegården)	90
Sun.	20	"	

DENMARK

Mon.	21	Copenhagen (Hotel d'Angleterre)	50
Tues.	22	"	
Wed.	23	"	
Thurs.	24	"	
Fri.	25	"	
Sat.	26	Svendborg via ferry from Korsør to Nyborg—Odense (Christiansminde Hotel)	90
Sun.	27	"	
Mon.	28	"	
Tues.	29	Ribe via ferry from Faaborg to Mommark—Tønder, Møgeltønder Rudebøl, Rømø Island (Riberhus)	100
Wed.	30	Ribe	
Thurs.	31	Aarhus via Vejle, Jelling, Silkeborg (Royal Hotel)	120

SEPTEMBER

Fri.	1	Hvidsten (Hvidsten Kro)	25
Sat.	2	Aalborg via Mariager, Rebild (night boat to Copenhagen)	40
Sun.	3	Copenhagen	
Mon.	4	"	
Tues.	5	New York (Scandinavian Airlines System via Iceland)	

By and large it was a good itinerary although, in the light of experience, we would make a few minor changes.

Two days in Oslo, for example, are not enough. We cut down our Oslo stay partly to fit into the limits of our time (never forgetting Sunday in Rättvik) and partly because we did not want to spend a midsummer Sunday in a strange city. It would probably have worked out better had we taken the Tuesday S.A.S. plane, instead of leaving New York on Thursday as we did. We could then have spent three days in Oslo and left Saturday morning.

Hotel accommodations in all three countries are excellent. The only difficulty is there are not enough of them. As a result the traveler in Scandinavia from June 15 to September 1 cannot drift whimsically along, stopping each night where his fancy pleases—unless he wants to spend it under the stars.

If you like a roof over your head, then you must choose your roof weeks in advance and make sure there is going to be room for you under it. In the big cities, substitute months for weeks. As for front rooms in the Grand Hotel in Stockholm, I have only met one couple who claim to have occupied one and I suspect them of exaggeration.

Bennett's Travel Bureau will not only make these reservations for you (through your travel agent in the United States) but will also issue neat little books of coupons—one for a room, one for a bath, another for breakfast, until each day and night has been accounted for. These are paid for at the start in one colossal lump sum which is frightfully painful at the moment but, once the loss has been absorbed by the subconscious, makes the rest of the trip seem free.

A glance at the Norwegian section of the itinerary will show much use of car ferries. We were told in the United States that there was always plenty of room on these ferries and that they ran frequently. Neither statement was correct. Some only run twice a day and during July they are jammed to capacity. Have the porter at your hotel make reservations several days in advance, if possible, or you may have your itinerary badly dislocated—and a dislocated itinerary, in Norway especially, can be as crippling as a dislocated knee.

I would make no changes in the Norwegian itinerary except between Geiranger and Trondheim. The route which we took through Åndalsnes and Dombås would have been interesting enough had it not been for the supercolossal scenery which preceded it. I would suggest the route by ferry and road from Geiranger to Molde and then from Molde by ferry and coast road to Trondheim. Certainly it could be done in the three days we took between Geiranger and Trondheim. Depending on the ferries it might be done in two, but although I have never been there, I have an idea that a little time in Molde would be rewarding. Anyone wishing to stick to our route should plan to go from Åndalsnes to Trondheim in one day. It is the only stretch we saw in Norway where I would dare suggest a 260-mile run.

The roads in Norway are excellent. In fact they are excellent in all three countries. On the other hand, the Norwegian roads are for the most part narrow; in places they would put a corkscrew to shame and many of them must have been engineered by mountain goats. They are not dangerous, however, the outer edges being protected by low concrete parapets or rocks. Wherever the going gets dizzy the speed limits in Norway are set very low. They could be abolished entirely and it would make no difference. No one has any desire to go fast in the mountain regions.

We went north from Trondheim to Verdalsöyra and there turned east to Sweden up the Verdal. We crossed Sweden to Sundsvall on the east coast, then down the coast to Gävle and inland to Rättvik.

It was not a particularly interesting trip and it took four days. I would suggest turning south at Östersund and going straight to Rättvik on the interior road or going south from Trondheim to

Röros, Norway, and entering Sweden by way of Fjällnäs. This road eventually ties into the Östersund-Rättvik road. By pushing a bit it should be possible to cover either route in two days, thus saving two days for more interesting places—and there are plenty of them. We could find out nothing about the condition of the road, so it is at your own risk, but we never saw a bad road in Scandinavia.

Our Swedish itinerary missed three great sections of the country that we wanted very much to visit, namely the western section lying between the Norwegian border and the lakes, the castle country in the southern tip, and the northwest coast from Göteborg to Norway. It was just another of those problems which used to drive us half-crazy when we were trying to fit an itinerary into a time schedule and it helped us to understand our Scandinavian friends who drew great circles on the map with their fingers and said "All that you should see."

The Swedish roads over which we traveled were excellent, both main and secondary.

There is little about our routing that we would have changed in Denmark. If we had had more time we would like to have explored the country south of Copenhagen and the big islands off the southern end of Zealand. Perhaps one day at Svendborg would have been sufficient. But those are small things.

In all three countries food varies from tops in the cities to excellent in the country districts. It is true that in Norway you may be conscious of a greater emphasis on fish than you are used to and, for those who prefer the pattern of accustomed things, a *koldt bord* breakfast in a Norwegian country hotel can be startling. Compared with what one would find on a similar loop of the United States, however, the Scandinavians win hands down.

We took our own car for two reasons. We knew that there were drive-yourself cars available in Oslo, Stockholm and Copenhagen, but the information about them was not sufficiently definite and we had no time to waste on misunderstandings when we reached Oslo. Also, we wanted to end the trip at Copenhagen and no one could explain just what we were to do with an Oslo car in Copenhagen.

Our second reason was that at the time of our trip most of the cars available for renting in the Scandinavian countries seemed to be English midget models or Swedish Volvos, and we wanted room for plenty of baggage in addition to our knees. This is of course a matter of temperament, and we have no quarrel with those who like to travel for eight weeks curled up like embryos, encased in nylon, and with a toothbrush stuck behind the ear.

We settled on a Plymouth suburban wagon. It had a 111-inch wheel base which made it easy to handle on the switchback mountain roads of Norway. Its broad seats were comfortable, and in the rear we had ample room for our highly assorted oddments of personal belongings.

To anyone used to doing four hundred miles a day in the United States some of our day's runs will seem short. On the west coast of Norway, however, where the roads go up and down as much as they go forward, a hundred miles is enough. The seventy-seven miles from Loen to Geiranger is one of the world's sensational drives and will fill up the day of the most ambitious motorist.

We had the greatest difficulty in obtaining road maps of sufficiently large scale. If Sweden, Norway and Denmark can co-operate sufficiently to create the Scandinavian Airlines System, it seems odd that to date they have not produced a system of uniform road maps. Perhaps they will have done so by the time this book is published.

We were unable to find an over-all road map of the three countries and, as each country produces maps drawn to different scales and (with the exception of Norway) devoid of any indication of distances between points, trip-planning is apt to be on the vague side.

The Norwegians have the best map. It is published by the Royal Norwegian Automobile Club and may be obtained through the Norwegian National Travel Office, Norway House, 290 Madison Avenue, New York City. It is on a scale of 1 : 1,000,000 and is reasonably easy to read. It might have been more so if the road directions and explanations on the inside of the cover had been in English as well as Norwegian.

At the Swedish National Travel Office in New York one may obtain a 1:1,500,000 scale map, which is good enough if one is sticking to the main roads, but is on too small a scale to give the detail of the secondary roads, nor does it give any indication of distances. A friend in the United States saved the situation for us by producing a large-scale Esso map in four sections, but we never saw another like it through the length and breadth of Sweden.

The Danish Travel Bureau publishes a gay little road map which again is excellent for over-all planning, but omits the secondary road system entirely. In view of the fact that much of the charm of Denmark lies hidden along its back roads, this is a deficiency. In this case also a friend sent us a large-scale Standard Oil map. It was very old and quite unreliable on the subject of secondary roads, but most comforting up to the point where it left us in a tangle of dirt lanes to work things out on our own.

I am sure that I will receive letters from various companies and associations telling me about the superb maps which they have published. They will undoubtedly be right, but if they existed when we were there they were treated as confidential.

There are just a few more items that might be of interest.

The Scandinavian laws on the subject of driving after drinking are tough. In Norway the law forbids a person to drive after having more than 1/20 of 1% of alcohol in the blood. Just how a motorist is supposed to know when that condition has been reached I do not know, but if a would-be driver approaches his car with an infantile toddle the police are apparently authorized to haul him off to the police station without further argument, and take a blood count.

In Sweden it is a criminal offense to operate an automobile with more than .002 (two *pro mille*) of alcohol in the blood stream. A good-sized *snaps* or a few glasses of beer will accomplish that. If an accident occurs, the driver is immediately whisked off to the nearest police station and if he fails to pass his examination a jail sentence, not transmutable to fines, follows without exception. It is a law which introduces an element of adventure in many Swedish lives.

In Denmark the laws are similar. We were told that they were strictly enforced, but people did not seem to be quite so worried about them as in Norway and Sweden.

Gasoline is plentiful, but expensive in all three countries. To compensate for this, however, the distances are so short compared to those we are accustomed to in the United States that the sting is drawn to a large extent.

As for repairs, we had few, but those were taken care of with a dispatch and efficiency that compared favorably with anything to be found in the United States; and the same might be said for the equipment of the repair shops.

The matter of clothes is a bit difficult. It can be chilly to cold on the west coast of Norway even in July and there was a nip in the late August air of Jutland. On the other hand, Sweden produced beautiful summer weather. It is best to be prepared for both. Bring a light overcoat, sports clothes and comfortable walking shoes.

The Scandinavians are conventional people in the matter of dress. If you are invited to dine at a private house you put on your best bib and tucker, although during the summer you can get away without a tuxedo. It is also well to remember that, being conventionalists, they do not dress up in comedy costumes when they take to the road or the beaches. We did not see a "play suit" or a Truman shirt in the length and breadth of Scandinavia and it made quite a pleasant change. If that gives you any help on "what to bring," make the most of it.

Anyone contemplating a Scandinavian trip should get in touch with the National Travel Offices of each country which are located in New York City. These are government agencies staffed with intelligent, efficient and agreeable gentlemen who will spare no efforts to be helpful. Your only difficulty will be that they are all so enthusiastic that you will want to spend your entire time in the country of the last one to whom you talk.

Their addresses in New York are:

> Norwegian National Travel Office
> Norway House
> 290 Madison Avenue
>
> Swedish National Travel Office
> 630 Fifth Avenue
>
> Danish National Travel Office
> 588 Fifth Avenue

Prospective visitors to Scandinavia who are interested in special aspects of Scandinavian culture will find it well worth while to get in touch with the American Scandinavian Foundation, 127 East 73rd Street, which for over forty years has fostered cultural and intellectual relations between the United States and Scandinavian countries.

Membership in the AAA is also a "must." They took charge

of the forwarding of our car; made it possible, through the Royal Norwegian Automobile Association, for us to be met at the plane in Oslo with our own car; furnished us much helpful information and made themselves generally indispensable.

There are a number of excellent books on the three countries. The two which embrace all of Scandinavia and which we used constantly were Sydney Clark's *All the Best in Scandinavia* (Dodd, Mead) and Clara F. Laughlin's *So You're Going to Scandinavia!* (Houghton, Mifflin). Neither of them ever left the front seat of the car and it is difficult to see how we could have planned the trip, or found our way about without them.

All the Best in Scandinavia is a mine of just the sort of information one needs in selecting stopping places, restaurants and a dozen other things. *So You're Going to Scandinavia!* has much of the same information, but we found it particularly useful for historical background information.

Other books and pamphlets which belong in your Scandinavian library are:

BOOKS

Fielding's Travel Guide to Europe		William Sloan Associates
Norway, Changing and Changeless	By Agnes Rothery	Viking Press
Norwegian Holiday	By Harlan Major	Funk & Wagnalls
Sweden, the Land and the People	By Agnes Rothery	Viking Press
Sweden, Model for a World	By Hudson Strode	Harcourt, Brace & Co.
Introduction to Sweden	By Ingvar Anderson	The Swedish Institute, Stockholm
Danish Delight	By Monica Redlich	Duckworth (London)
Denmark is a Lovely Land	By Hudson Strode	Harcourt, Brace & Co.
Tourist in Denmark		*Politiken*, Copenhagen

PAMPHLETS

"Motoring in Norway"	Norway Travel Association
"Motoring in Sweden"	Royal Swedish Automobile Club

"Facts about Sweden"	Forum, Stockholm
"How to Feel at Home in Sweden"	Swedish Tourist Traffic Association
"We Danes and You"	The National Travel Association of Denmark
"Facts About Denmark"	*Politiken,* Copenhagen
"This Copenhagen"	Paul Fenneberg

These are merely a few that drifted across our path. There are many more, in addition to innumerable books of pictures and travel folders, most of which are decoratively uninformative.

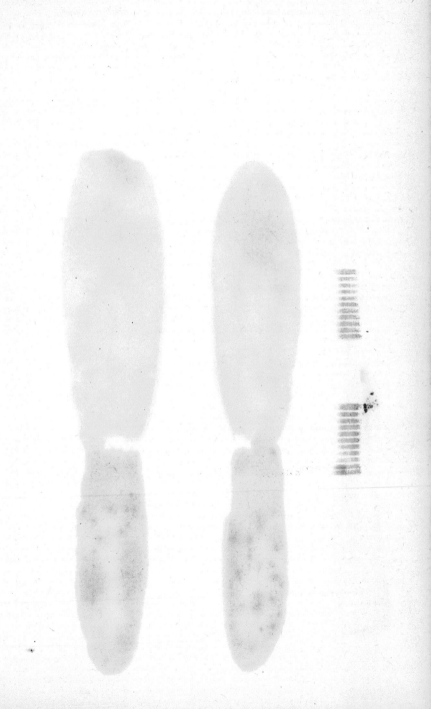